CHAMPIONS NEVER QUIT

CHAMPIONS NEVER QUIT

GOD IS CLOSE BY YOUR SIDE

TIMOTHY MCGAFFIN II

Copyright © 2013 Timothy John McGaffin II
Permission to quote from this publication is granted provided due acknowledgement is made.

Published by
Timothy John McGaffin II

www.ChampionsNeverQuit.com

Paperback ISBN 978-0-615-84590-6
Hardcover ISBN 979-8-218-14109-7

Designed by
Timothy John McGaffin II

Photo credits:
Pages 224, 225, 228, 229, back cover;
Ryan Houston Photography.
Pages 232, 233, 235, 237;
McGaffin Family Photos.

CONTENTS

1	THE DREAM	1
2	THE TRIUMPH	5
3	NEVER GIVE UP!	10
4	SIMPLIFY FOR SUCCESS	16
5	GOD IS CLOSE BY (PRAYER)	20
6	KEEP PRAYING	42
7	NEVER NEVER GIVE UP!	73
8	"I'LL BE THERE"	92
9	KEEP HAVING FUN	152
10	GOD IS VICTORY	195
11	PETE CUMMINGS: THE GREATEST EVER	199
12	MAMA: THE GREATEST EVER	206
13	POPPY: THE GREATEST EVER	212
14	NEVER NEVER NEVER GIVE UP!	218
	THIS IS IT!	225

CHAPTER 1

THE DREAM

Never never never never never never quit.

You are a child of God, a son or daughter of a Heavenly King and Queen. God is with you, answers all of your prayers and makes all of your dreams come true. God never gives you a dream or a wish without also giving you the power to make your dream or wish come true.

My dream to play basketball came to me as an answer to my prayers from Heavenly Father.

Sometimes you will achieve your dream quickly, sometimes slowly, and sometimes it will appear or seem like your dream will never come true. Remember that God works in mysterious ways, at least mysterious to us while traveling through our mortal journey. Your dream will become a reality no matter what the situation may appear like at a certain time, as long as you keep exercising faith in God. Even death is just an illusion because there is no death in Heaven.

I prayed when I was little and asked Heavenly Father to help me know what I should do and be when I grew up. I also wanted to be the best there ever was at whatever it was, I am supposed to be or do. So I also asked God to help me become the best there ever was.

I received the answer to my prayer one day soon after turning nine years old. God truly answered me by the power of the still small voice. The answer was that I should play basketball.

Heavenly Father gave me my dream of playing basketball and to become the greatest basketball player ever and promised me that He would help me and I would not fail.

Yes, you read that correctly, I did just say "the greatest basketball player ever." I thought to myself that in order for me to become the best player there ever was I am going to need to play in the NBA (National Basketball Association) because that is where all the best players in the world play. I knew making the NBA would be extremely difficult because it is almost impossible to play professional basketball, especially in the NBA. The only way I would be successful in making it to the NBA is if God helped me. If I do my best, if I do everything I can possibly do within my control, God will do the rest that I cannot do for myself.

With God helping you close by your side there is no way you will fail in making your dream come true...

I tried out for the basketball team when I was

THE DREAM

thirteen years old in seventh grade at Lakeridge Junior High School:
   ...I failed to make the team.

I tried out again for the basketball team in eighth grade at Canyon View Junior High School:
   ...I failed.

I tried out again in ninth grade at Canyon View:
   ...I failed.

I tried out again in tenth grade at Orem High School:
   ...I failed.

I tried out again in eleventh grade at Timpanogos High School:
   ...I failed.

I tried out again in twelfth grade at American Fork High School:
   ...I failed.

About four and a half years later I tried out again at Utah Valley State College:
   ...I failed.

I tried out again at the University of Utah:
   ...I failed.

I tried out again the next year at the University of Utah:

...the assistant basketball coach, Eric Jackson, called me into his office...

The greatest power in the universe is: to get back up, to come back, to bounce back, to try again, to rise again, to keep going, to keep moving, to reappear, to redeem, to repent, to return or most simply, to "never give up" or "never quit".

Coming back my whole life for this moment, despite all the pain, heartache and failure: Here I am.

I'm back again.

Taking a seat in his office, Jackson expressed his gratitude for me. He explained how impressed he was with how hard I trained again these last twelve months.

He reminded me there is only one open spot on the team. Only one. Every year before there was more than one spot available but not this year.

"You were our number two man," he said.

...I failed.

CHAPTER 2

THE TRIUMPH

Remember, God never gives you a dream or a wish without also giving you the power to make your dream or wish come true.

About three weeks later on Thursday November 13, before the second preseason game for the University of Utah of the 2003-2004 season, we took our dining room seats at the The Marriott University Park hotel for our pregame meal.

The players, the majority of the coaching staff and myself, —since I was one of the equipment managers— ate in relative silence. As we were focusing our thoughts and preparing our minds for the upcoming game tonight, a voice next to me broke through the quiet, speaking directly to me but meant to garner the attention and be heard by everyone.

Usually a voice of leadership, this time however it was a mocking voice, intent on putting me down in front of everyone.

This particular player said, taunting me, that the coaches were not telling me the truth, that they were lying to me about how I was their second choice because they did not want to hurt my feelings.

"Nope, I was the second choice," I quickly interjected defiantly to set the record straight.

He said I would never be able to become a college basketball player because it is almost impossible. "You want to be where we are, you want to be one of us, but you'll never be one of us. It's too hard," he said.

Palpable silence filled the room as everyone anticipated what I was going to say or if I was going to say anything at all in response to the words of one of the most important players on the team.

"You're right," I said as he seemed surprised I agreed, "it is almost impossible to play basketball in college, —to become a college basketball player."

"And as difficult as it is to play basketball in college, it is even more difficult or even more impossible to play basketball in the NBA."

"But I have done something that is so difficult, that not a single person in this room has done what I've done."

Shock, disbelief, or curiosity at this moment were all apparent to one degree or another as everyone in this deeply silent dining room tried to figure out what could I possibly be talking about?

I kept going:

"And not only has no one in this room done what I've done, but what I have done is so difficult, that, not even a single player in ALL of college basketball has done what I've done."

"And not only has no one playing in college done what I've done, but also not even a single basketball player in ALL of the NBA has done what I've done."

"And not only has no one in college or the NBA done what I've done, but not a single college or NBA basketball player PAST or PRESENT has done what I've done."

"What I have done is:
No one has ever tried out to make a basketball team as many times in a row as I have and also failed as many times in a row as I have and STILL HAS NOT GIVEN UP."

I quickly counted off the number of failed attempts in chronological order, seventh through twelfth grades and three more attempts so far at the college level, summarizing that so far I had now tried to make the basketball team nine consecutive times over a period of twelve years.

"The main reason you're on the team is because you just happened to grow to be seven feet tall. You didn't choose to be seven feet tall. It just happened," I said to him.

"The door has always been opened for you. But the door has always been closed for me and yet I still keep choosing to continue to move forward by reopening the door every time it shuts on me."

I asked him, "If you would have failed to make your high school team one year would you have come back and tried out again to make the team a second time?"

"Uh, yeah, you probably would have tried again," I said, answering my own question I just posed to him.

I then asked him if he would have failed two years in a row, would he have come back to do his best to try out again a third time in a row?

"Hmm, maybe," I said, answering again my own question to him.

"—And I know without a doubt you would not have come back to try again a fourth time."

I explained to him and everyone else in the room that I failed to make the basketball team nine consecutive times. Nine times. But I have come back nine consecutive times. Nine times. I still have not given up. I still have not quit.

"I know the most difficult thing you can do in your life is to never quit or to get back up when you get knocked down."

"And not only is 'never quitting' the MOST DIFFICULT thing you can do in your life, it is also the GREATEST thing you can do in your life; and I know the only types of people capable of 'never quitting' are champions. A champion is the greatest type of person you can become."

CHAPTER 3

NEVER GIVE UP!

Playing basketball in the NBA, or in college or anything else that might be seen as "great" in the eyes of the world is NOTHING compared to the power of the person who never gives up.

There is a difference between trying your best and doing your best. Nothing can stop you from doing your best! No one can stop you from doing your best! You are unstoppable if you want to be.

It is the effort that matters and it is the effort that God cares about. Do your best and God will do the rest, and you will be exactly where you are currently meant to be. Victory will be yours!

When you come back, failure is turned into triumph, negative is turned into positive, wounds are healed, mistakes are erased, sins are forgiven, and weak things are made strong. God redeems you when you come back.

Now for a moment let me quickly go back to the

end of that entire exchange with that particular player and the team in the dining room. After I said to everybody that the most difficult and greatest thing you can do is to get back up when you get knocked down and only champions can do it, there was one last thing I said.

Finally, I said to everyone in the room:
"Now, I haven't talked to every person in the world but I'm pretty sure I'm the only one in the world to have tried out and failed to make a basketball team as many times in a row as I have without giving up."

The team captain and team leader, Nick Jacobson, then spoke up and said:
"I think you're right Tim. I think you are the only one in the world."
"Yeah, thanks Nick," I softly replied in gratitude.
The room felt heavy quiet for what seemed like a long time as myself and others thought about what had been revealed to each of us.
The words I spoke were my words but they were also given to me somehow through the still small voice of God. Everything I said just came to me as I felt like God was close by my side somehow. My heart was on fire with the light and truth and nothing could stop me from letting it out and letting it shine.
It is my prayer that with God's help the words in this book are written accurately and communicated

correctly so that the message and testimony of "never quitting" is not misunderstood. I ask for your help to please have a prayer in your heart as you read so that the truth will triumph.

I am not boasting of myself. I am not saying I am better than anyone else or that life is a competition to raise ourselves above others while putting our fellow brothers and sisters down below us. I mean exactly the opposite of these things.

I am boasting not of myself but of God. God truly is with each one of us on a very personal level because each of us is truly a child of God.

There is no way I could have gotten back up that many times in a row without God helping me.

Never would I have kept coming back again and again, year after year, if it was not for the fact that Heavenly Father answered my prayer and told me He would help me become the greatest basketball player ever. If God did not answer my prayer, if He did not promise me that He would help me then I would not have made the choice to be unstoppable; I would have stopped a long time ago.

Actually, there is no way I could have gotten back up even just one time without God helping me.

It is not the amount of times you get back up that is important. It is not a competition to see who can rise back up the most that makes one great. All that matters is that you get back up.

All that matters is that you get back up each time you get knocked down, each time you fall, each time you fail, each time you make a mistake, each time you feel hurt, each time you get hit. Whether one time or countless times, just get back up each time and let your light shine.

Every return is equally great because every return brings you back to the top. You cannot get higher than highest. You cannot be greater than greatest. Once you return to the top, you are the top.

Yet the fact I came back so many times in a row proves that coming back is the most difficult thing you can ever do. And that fact proves that coming back cannot be done without God helping you.

The gospel is not a competition. The gospel is about doing your best by getting back up when you get knocked down and God will do the rest.

Getting back up is the greatest power in the universe and cannot be done without God giving you that power, because God, who created the universe, is that greatest power.

Getting back up is a divine action. It is faith in God and faith is action in God. Getting back up is the light that shines in the darkness, and the darkness comprehendeth it not. It is doing the impossible. It is the greatest power in the universe. It is the power of God.

What exactly is faith? Faith is being faithful, being faithful to God. Faith is "never giving up" on God, that the dark times will last but a small moment when compared to eternity, that the hard times will be overcome with the help of God who has overcome all obstacles. Faith is action in God, a divine action also called: "Never give up"!

Seeing is not believing. Seeing is in exercising faith and exercising faith is believing. The proof, the truth, or "seeing" is in the journey or in "exercising faith".

Life is not a competition with others but rather a competition with ourselves to simply do our best. We should not get satisfaction in beating another person but rather in beating the odds, in beating the darkness, in beating evil, in inspiring another person to simply do their best too. We should get satisfaction in giving our best effort. Victory!

It is no great feat to cheat. So-called "winners" who cheat do not really win anything when they deceive the world for a moment.

The effort, however, can never be cheated. The effort can never be deceived. You either give your best effort or you do not.

When you give your best effort and the world does not see it, it does not change the truth that you did give your best effort.

Two plus two does not equal five no matter how many times the world says it does or how many people says it equals five. Just because something is "popular" does not necessarily mean that it is true or right.

Do not worry if there were times that you did not do your best. The world wants you to worry and to think that you cannot come back. Do not listen to the lies. Every single person has had times when the effort was lacking. What matters is that you do your best now and come back to the very top. Do not procrastinate. Make the comeback now.

> "The greatest accomplishment is not in never falling, but in rising again after you fall."
> –Vince Lombardi

This is the great test of life, to see if we will do our best not just in the good times but also —and especially— in the bad times. When the hard and difficult times appear, this is the time not to shrink but to shine! This is the time to triumph! This is your time. This is your time to shine.

This Is It!

CHAPTER 4

SIMPLIFY FOR SUCCESS

The root meaning of the word "succeed" or "success" simply means to follow through or to finish.

> "Success is failure turned inside out, the silver tint of the clouds of doubt, and you can never tell how close you are, it may be near when it seems so far. So stick to the fight when you are hardest hit. It's when things seem worse, that you must not quit." –Unknown

When you succeed, you are a success.

When you follow through (succeed), you cross the finish (success) line.

Rising again after the fall is the most difficult thing you can ever do and at the same time it is also the most simple. It is not the most easy but it is the most simple.

There is a difference between simple and easy.

"Simple" is defined as that which is easy to understand by identifying the basic fundamentals.

"Easy" is defined as that which is simple to do by doing the basic fundamentals.

Simple makes easy.

If you want to climb the highest mountain, first simplify the climb into the basic fundamental steps which then makes it easy to follow through on each step by step to the top or to the finish.

Simplify for success.

Obstacles will appear along the pathway to the top of your personal mountain trying to stop you from following through by increasing the difficulty to simplify. Storms will rage, lightning, thundering, heat, cold, wind, rain, snow, ice, landslides, doubt, confusion, discouragement, frustration and darkness will appear to try and convince you that it is too hard to keep going step by step.

Along the path of my basketball journey I simplified the journey down to its basic steps to make it easier to succeed. When an obstacle appeared trying to prevent me from stepping any further, by increasing the difficulty to simplify, I then simplified the steps down even more to receive even more power to follow through and overcome the obstacle. The more you simplify, the easier it gets because the more your power increases. Or in other words when the obstacles appeared I prayed and asked God, who is the source of the power, to help me.

For example, when the storms appeared I went to the basic fundamentals of praying or pondering in my mind certain questions so I could receive the answers and therefore receive increased power needed to follow through.

Does God live? I know God lives. How do I know? God lives because when I do good I feel good, when I do bad I feel bad. Since there is good and evil and since I have a conscience then there is a God. If there was not a God then there would be no good and evil, there would be no feelings, there would be nothing.

I know God answered my prayer and gave me my dream to play basketball. How do I know God answered my prayer? It was not my imagination, it was real, it was the still small voice speaking to my heart. I felt it. I felt God close by me somehow.

Since God answered my prayer, then God is with me. Since God is with me I cannot fail. I cannot fail because God is all-powerful. God is all-powerful because God has overcome all obstacles. God has overcome all obstacles because God is unstoppable. God is unstoppable because God is the light that shines in darkness and the darkness comprehendeth it not.

Since I cannot fail because God is with me then why have I failed to make the basketball team so many times? I don't know yet. But I do know that God cannot lie. God cannot lie because God is truth. There must be something I need to learn. I will keep a positive attitude. God will reveal the miracle when it is supposed to be revealed. God will make my dream come true. I will not give up.

I stepped over the obstacle and kept moving forward.

Getting back up is the most difficult, greatest, most simple, and also the most easy thing you can do once you understand you simply need to put one foot in front of the other.

> "Life is strange with its twists and turns, as everyone of us sometimes learns. And many a failure turns about, when he might have won had he stuck it out. Don't give up though the race seems slow, you may succeed if you go on and go." –Anonymous

CHAPTER 5

GOD IS CLOSE BY (PRAYER)

John Stockton dribbled up the court with great quickness and urgency. Karl Malone positioned himself near the hoop with great skill and urgency. Stockton expertly timed the bounce pass down to the "Mailman" as Malone simultaneously caught the basketball and urgently made his move to the basket to deliver two more points for the Utah Jazz.

I thought to myself that the Jazz are really playing hard so they must be on the verge of winning the game before time runs out.

The score came up on the television screen showing only a couple minutes remaining in the game and to my confusion the Jazz were losing to the Los Angeles Lakers by a large double-digit deficit.

There was not enough time left to score enough points to come back from being down so far.

I thought to myself, "Why would the Jazz keep playing so hard if they don't have any chance to win the game?"

I first started watching NBA basketball a little bit when I was eight years old during the 1987-1988 season and the best team to me was the LA Lakers which included Magic Johnson, Kareem Abdul-Jabbar, James Worthy, and Byron Scott.

The Utah Jazz, which included John Stockton, Karl Malone, Mark Eaton, Thurl Bailey and Bobby Hansen were working hard to learn and become the best team themselves. The Jazz wanted to be the best like the Lakers.

Every game Stockton and Malone and the rest of the Jazz played the Lakers this season the Jazz got beaten very badly.

I had missed the rest of this specific game earlier and only caught the last couple minutes once I turned on the television. I thought initially because we were playing with so much focus, determination and urgency that maybe this time was going to be the first time that we were on the verge of beating the Lakers until the score appeared on the screen.

The effort I saw, despite being down by so much with no chance of winning, really stayed with me. I kept thinking to myself, "why would they play so hard at the end of the fourth quarter as if they were just about to win when they had no chance of winning?"

Later in the same season the Jazz and Lakers met again in a playoff game in Salt Lake City. This time when I turned on the television the Jazz were playing with the exact same level of focus, determination and urgency as before when the Jazz lost so badly to the Lakers. Again the score appeared on the television screen and this time the Jazz were miraculously beating the Lakers by more than twenty points. I could not believe we were winning by such a large margin when every other time we were blown out by the Lakers. I had to look at the score multiple times to make sure I was really seeing it correctly.

"Usually we're the ones getting blown out by the Lakers but this time we're the ones blowing them out!" ...I thought to myself in amazement as I kept jumping up and down!

I learned it does not matter what the score is, what matters is the effort. To do your best when you are up is one thing but to do your best when you are down is the true victory.

Despite being blown out at the end of the first game, Stockton and Malone and the rest of the Jazz did not give up and continued to play as hard as they possibly could until they finished the game. They could have just given in and accepted defeat before the game was over and just went through the motions with a lackadaisical effort. But instead they played as if they were just about to win. They may not have won in the eyes of the world the first time but that winning effort carried over to the next time when the Jazz blew out the Lakers resulting in a miraculous win. The effort between the first loss to the second win was no different. Both times it was the same winning effort. You never lose when you do your best. Do your best and

God will do the rest by working and revealing the miracle.

There is something to be said for those of us who continue to fight on with all our hearts at the end of our own personal fourth quarters even when it appears all hope may be lost. What it says to me is that you are a champion. Champions have faith in God and are victorious.

About three years earlier when I was about five years old I knew nothing about basketball and I was instead taking piano lessons.

I was dreading growing up because I did not want to enter the adult world. To be an adult meant to me that I would be forced to do things I did not want to do and be someone I was not. So many adults I met when I was little always seemed to me to be so stressed out and unhappy.

I did not want to grow up to play the piano because I did not want to be someone I was not, I did not want to be fake, I did not want to be a slave basically. I liked the piano and I liked music but I did not like the image I imagined in my mind that I thought the adult world wanted me to be. I imagined that I would have to coverup my hair and be forced to wear a fake white-haired curly wig like I saw in old paintings or pictures of composers like Mozart from past centuries. I did not want to wear tight restricting dress-up clothes with choking shirt collars and irritating dress coats with long heavy coattails. And I thought I would have to play boring songs that the other adults would request me to play; that I could not play the fun songs I would want to play since most adults seemed to like boring, uninspiring music.

I remember talking to myself and thinking it would be about thirteen more years until I had to worry about being an adult since I was already five and thought most people are considered adults at eighteen.

"Well, I have about thirteen more years before I have to really worry about it," I once said out loud quietly to myself.

One day when I was again pondering about this problem of having to grow up and being someone I did not want to be, a familiar voice came to my heart and said to me:

"You do not have to be anyone you do not want to be. You can choose to be anyone you want to be. And I will help you."

It was Heavenly Father speaking to me. I do not know exactly how it works but I know it was Heavenly Father speaking to me in a real voice, a still voice I could not hear with my physical ears but felt somehow with my heart.

Once I excitedly realized it was true that I could choose to do and be anything I wanted, I started brainstorming ideas of what I wanted!

Maybe I do want to play the piano? Now I know I do not have to let the adults make me into something I'm not. I can play fun music, I can wear what I want, I can get creative and do things musically that have not been done before. I do not have to play the piano like everyone else.

I kept thinking...

"What do I really want?"

I initially came up with two requirements to help me choose what I wanted to do and be. First, whatever I eventually choose, it has to be fun! I don't want to be living a life of drudgery like those stressed-out unhappy adults I see. I want to be free, I want to have fun. Second, it has to be something where I can help people. Later after more thought, I added a third requirement to my list. Third, I have to be the best there ever was at whatever I choose to be.

I know God was the one who helped inspire me to come up with these three ideas or requirements that would help me find my dream.

I wanted to be the best because Heavenly Father said He would help me and since God is the best why wouldn't He also help me to be like He is? Second place is less than first and I don't want to be less than first. And God doesn't want us to be less than first or less than complete either. Next I thought I wouldn't actually be happy though if I was the best and no one else was.

So I asked myself, while directing my question toward Heaven, "Can we all be the best?"

My mind went to thinking about Jesus and realizing that Jesus already is the greatest. Since Jesus already is the greatest, then I guess we cannot all be the best as well then. When I thought this however, I knew my thinking that we cannot all be the best as well, was incorrect because God loves each of us like He loves His Son, Jesus and would want all of us to be the greatest since we all are sons and daughters of God.

To be continued:

The gospel of liberty!
The choice is up to each one of us. We can be anything or anyone we choose to be and God will help each of us if we want His help. God will never force us to do anything or be anyone we do not choose ourselves.
Liberty of conscience, liberty of thought, liberty of speech and religious liberty for all!
Before I continue, I again ask for your help to please keep that prayer in your heart so that the truth triumphs. My concern is that the personal experiences I have begun to share involving God, and will continue to share, might be misunderstood and thereby frustrate the truth from being received. Misunderstandings might occur because not everyone calls God by the same name or the religion they follow the same. Although we may call God by a different name or have different religious views at a given time, our differences should not frustrate the truth but rather it should reveal the truth. If we can agree there is good and evil, right and wrong, truth and error; that the God we wor-

ship and the religion we follow should be what is good and right and true then we are united in seeking after what is good, right and true. Being united in seeking the truth removes the obstacles impeding the way allowing each of us to receive and learn more truth.

The God I worship and the religion I follow is truth and liberty. The gospel of Jesus Christ is the gospel of liberty. Liberty of conscience! Liberty of thought! Liberty of speech! And religious liberty for all!

Liberty means that we have free agency so we are free to choose to be and do whatever we want as long as we do not hurt other people. There are false definitions of liberty given by the wolves in sheep's clothing who want us to falsely believe that liberty means we can do whatever we want including hurting other people. Hurting other people is not liberty, it is tyranny and slavery. As long as we each seek after the truth we will find it and "the truth shall make you free." (John 8:32) True religion is liberty. Anything that infringes on your personal liberty is false religion. There has never been an evil thing done in the name of true religion. Anything evil done in the name of religion is done in the name of false religion by the wolves in sheep's clothing who make evil appear good and good appear evil.

I ask for your help by keeping that prayer in your heart so that the light and truth is discerned from the darkness. My sincere prayer is that by sharing my light it increases your light the same way others like yourself who share their light increases my light. All of our lights shine brighter the more we help each other. Let your God-given gifts and talents shine, let your light shine! In shining your light, the darkness gets exposed and the truth ultimately triumphs! The final victory will be for liberty. We are all in this as a team. Just like in basketball, we can only win the championship by helping each other and having fun together as a team. Victory is ours.

Continuing:

I narrowed my choices of what I wanted to do down to three options: Artist, policeman, or fireman. All three met my inspired requirements of being fun, being able to help people and then being something I would want to be the best there ever was.

As an artist I could have fun doing something I really loved, such as drawing and painting, and I could help others by inspiring them through my art. However, I knew most artists —even the best ones, do not really make enough income to live on. I did not care about money but I did care about making enough to support my family. I decided I would be an artist but that it would not be my career.

Between policeman and fireman, my mind went back and forth a lot. Neither one was going to pay much but they would at least pay enough. Both I could definitely help people and helping people is a lot of fun. Ultimately I chose not to be a policeman because I thought there was a chance I might get shot. I did not want my wife and our children to be worried everyday about me getting hurt. So the last choice that remained was fireman. Being a fireman is also dangerous like a policeman but the danger is usually more controlled since I would not need to worry about defending myself against the criminal element that a policeman would.

"I'm going to be a fireman," I said out loud to myself. I made my decision.

I started developing a plan in my mind on how I would begin my training to become the best fireman there ever was. I thought to myself that it is better to start training now when I'm little than to wait until I'm older since all of this extra time will really be an advantage to perfect the skills I need to be the best fireman ever.

"No, that's not it. It just doesn't feel right," I said to myself after some days went by. I just didn't feel in my heart being a fireman was really what I was supposed to do.

I now felt like I was starting all over again. I felt confused on how I was going to figure out my dream.

As I pondered in my mind on how I was going to figure out what I wanted to do, my mind again went back to remembering how Heavenly Father told me He would help me. Next I focused on my parents, Mama and Poppy, and how they always taught me how to pray and ask Heavenly Father for help with all things.

Every night we prayed together as a family and

afterward we would kiss each other goodnight. My parents taught me and my younger sister, Pollyanna and my younger brother, Patrick to do our personal prayers everyday too.

I knew I needed to pray and ask Heavenly Father to help me to know what I should do.

I knelt down and prayed:
"Dear Heavenly Father, please help me to know what I should do when I grow up. I don't know what I should do but I know that you will help me. Please help me to know what I want to do. Please help me to know what my dreams are."

When I finished praying I felt good because I knew Heavenly Father had listened to me.

I waited for an answer.

I did not recognize any specific answer other than that I felt good and knew my prayer had been received.

I was about seven years old when I prayed specifically to receive an answer on what I should do when I grow up.

I kept praying every single day without fail for more than a year without ever receiving a specific answer. Even though I still had not received a clear answer, each time I prayed I knew Heavenly Father had heard me and because He heard me I knew I would receive the answer when I was meant to.

Shortly after turning nine years old in late August of 1988, I started third grade at Scera Park Elementary. My family was living in Orem, Utah a few miles away from Provo Canyon. Our next door neighbors, Brother and Sister Westenskow, (we call our neighbors who attend church with us by Brother and Sister) had a long narrow strip of rose bushes they removed alongside their driveway and filled in with concrete on Labor Day of that year; the first Monday of September. They installed a basketball hoop into the concrete, transforming their driveway into a basketball court. The following Saturday, after the new concrete driveway finished drying, I really wanted to play on their new basketball court for some reason.

I had only shot a basketball once before in my life and that was about six months earlier in the spring of second grade during a recess at school. I was into drawing and creating art and not really into playing sports like most of the other kids in my neighborhood. One of the older kids from my neighborhood gave me one chance to shoot his mini basketball and my one shot made contact with nothing but sky. I stood just a few feet away and didn't know how to shoot so when I threw the ball it went flying way over the top of the fourteen-foot-high backboard. That was my first and only attempt ever to shoot a basketball.

Now about six months later on this cloudy fall day I suddenly felt a desire to play basketball on this driveway next door.

There were some old deflated basketballs from

my dad lying around in our outdoor shed from when he played basketball. I picked one out and imagined an invisible hoop sitting on the edge of the roof of our carport. I began to toss the basketball up on top of the roof attempting to make shots through the invisible rim of the invisible basket. After shooting like this for a while my parents came outside to see what was going on since they must have heard the thuds of the ball hitting the roof. I told them I wanted to play basketball but I was too shy to ask the Westenskow family if I could play on their new court. My parents went next door with me and asked. After I got permission to play, my dad helped me bring one of his flat deflated basketballs back to life with enough air so it would bounce properly again.

"This is fun!", I thought to myself as I tried to somehow make another shot.

It was just me, the basket and the ball.

Just me and the rhythm.

The rhythmic sounds of the ball bouncing off the pavement, the backboard, the rim; the ball swishing through the net of the basket. The rhythmic sounds of my feet and my shoes moving across the pavement, the rhythmic sounds of the dance.

Just me and the feeling.

The feeling of fun and the thrill of making a basket, of grabbing a missed shot and trying again; the feeling of the dance, the feeling of the rhythm.

I felt that familiar voice coming into my heart again.

"I think this might be the answer to my prayer," I said to myself as I realized how much fun I was having.

I stopped playing.

God is close by.

I stood there on the driveway, alone in quiet, asking myself —while directing my thoughts toward Heaven— "Is this the answer to my prayer?"

Rather than receiving any specific words, at least not any words I could recognize, I instead received specific thoughts into my heart and mind.

My mind went back to my three inspired requirements for helping me to determine what I wanted to be: first, it has to be fun; second, it has to be something where I can help people; third, something I would want to be the best there ever was.

I visualized playing basketball and how much fun it would be; and I thought about how I would be able to get paid to play. Getting paid to do anything you love, especially playing a game, would be a dream come true. I didn't care about money but I did care about being able to support my wife and our children of course.

Playing basketball would definitely be fun but maybe too much fun because I wouldn't really be able to help people by playing a game, I thought.

"But how can I help people by playing basketball?", I asked Heavenly Father in my mind.

At this precise moment of asking, my mind saw John Stockton urgently dribbling the basketball up the hardwood court, perfectly timing the bounce pass to his teammate Karl Malone just as the "Mailman" was establishing position, who then urgently turned hard to the basket to speedily deliver two more points in the final minutes of the race. Even though Stockton and Malone and their Utah Jazz teammates were down by what seemed like an insurmountable deficit in the final stretch of a game against the LA Lakers, the Jazz kept playing just as hard as if they were on the verge of winning; they simply would not quit.

"That's how I can help people by playing basketball," I enthusiastically said to myself. "I can help other people by inspiring them to not give up just like they (John Stockton, Karl Malone and the Utah Jazz) inspired me to not give up."

To do your best when you are down, even if it appears all hope of winning may be lost, is the true test and the true victory; it's the heart of a champion. It's the effort that matters. It's the effort that God cares about. Finish the race victorious.

My mind then moved to quickly remember two more basketball moments. The first of these two was when Michael Jordan kept making the same fadeaway jump shot over and over, again and again from the exact same spot on the floor. The Chicago Bulls were playing at home against the Detroit Pistons in a playoff game. I got the feeling the Bulls had been beaten a lot by the Pistons like the Jazz had been beaten a lot by the Lakers. The Bulls were trailing the Pistons by a few points and were trying to make a comeback with the crowd very enthusiastically cheering their team on. I had no idea who Michael Jordan was. My dad turned the game on the television and told me that this guy was supposed to be good. I just remember Jordan taking that exact same fadeaway jump shot repeatedly because it could not be stopped and I remember the crowd really putting their whole hearts and souls into cheering their team on and really being the reason for the comeback. The cheers of the fans energized everyone and made everyone believe that winning was possible and close at hand.

The third basketball sequence my mind saw was Larry Bird playing basketball. I hadn't really seen Bird play yet in any particular game. I had only seen a couple brief highlights of him and my dad said something about him a couple times. And from just those highlight plays I recognized Bird possessed masterful basketball skills, technique, and teamwork. I could see and recognize he was someone who worked really hard and simply loved playing basketball with all of his heart and I wanted to also do something with all of my heart.

Lastly, I visualized myself training, practicing and working as hard as I possibly could and relying and trusting in God to help me every step of the way and never ever giving up until I made my dream of playing basketball come true.

I imagined myself playing basketball against the best players in the world and with the best teammates in the world. I imagined the hard times that would come and visualized myself praying and asking God for help to overcome these times. I visualized the people I would come in contact with cheering me on to keep going and myself cheering on others to also keep going; cheering each other on to keep going after each of our dreams until we each triumph to make our dreams come true.

"Yes, this is the answer to my prayer," I said to myself. "This is it. This is my dream. My dream is to play basketball and become the best basketball player ever."

Again, I directed my thoughts toward Heavenly Father and asked for confirmation to make sure I was understanding Him correctly that this is really the answer to my prayer and really my dream?

"Yes. And I will help you. I will be there," came the still reply directly from Heavenly Father that I quietly felt in my heart.

I stood there on the driveway, in stillness, thinking about what just happened, about how simple the answer to my prayer came after such a long time, about being thankful that my prayer was answered and then making the commitment to myself and to God: I promise no matter what happens I will never never never give up, until my dream comes true.

Urgently I went inside to tell my parents, Mama and Poppy, I found out my dream is to play basketball in the NBA and that I knew this was my dream because Heavenly Father answered my prayer. I didn't tell them my dream was to become the best basketball player ever yet though because I knew making the NBA was almost impossible by itself and decided to take things one step at a time. First, I should focus on a plan to make the NBA and after I make it I can focus on becoming the best player ever.

    I had no delusions of the difficulty of the journey at hand, I knew it was going to be extremely difficult to make the NBA, basically impossible. I knew the only way I could make it is if God helped me. This is precisely why I earlier visualized in my mind praying and asking God for help to overcome the hard times when they would come. I knew that in order for God to perform the miracle I would need to do my part, I would need to do my best, do everything that is in my control and the thing that is entirely in my control is my effort. Nothing can stop me from giving my best effort. No one can stop me from giving my best effort. All I have to do is never quit and God will do the rest.

    My dad immediately started telling me about Larry Bird and how Bird would practice basketball every day for six hours. So I decided that if I really wanted to make it to the NBA I would need to do what the best players do. If you want to be the best, you need to learn from the best.

    My dad started telling me more as well about when he played basketball in high school and college and in the Army. He never really said anything before. I didn't really know he played basketball aside from seeing the flat deflated balls lying around in the shed and from just a few comments he made when watching parts of a few NBA games last winter and spring.

My dad also taught me how to correctly shoot a basketball and instructed me to always focus on keeping my elbow straight.

First, visualize yourself making the shot; believe that you are going to make it, keeping your eyes focused on the rim which is your target. Second, keep your balance and square your shoulders to evenly face the basket. Third, rest the ball on the palm of your hand with your fingertips bearing the weight and place your other hand on the side of the ball for balance. Fourth, make sure your elbow is always lined up straight with the basket and keep it straight as you release the ball from your hand and keep it straight as you follow through until the ball successfully goes through the hoop.

A common mistake shooters make is they don't keep their elbow straight so it makes it harder to make shots with a crooked elbow. Keep your elbow straight and follow through.

There's no time to procrastinate.

The time for action is now.

I immediately made a plan to practice basketball after school for six hours everyday just like Larry Bird. If I want to be the best I need to do what the best do.

The first skill I planned to develop and practice on would be my shooting. I wanted to perfect my shot to be able to make a higher percentage than anyone else in the NBA. To me, Larry Bird was the best shooter and he had to be the best because he practiced six hours a day so that is what I also need to do.

As soon as I arrived home after school I went next door to the driveway hoop of the Westenskows and began to practice shooting at around 3:45 in the afternoon, always focusing on keeping my elbow straight. I felt very awkward but I kept practicing until it was time to eat dinner. As soon as I finished eating I went right back outside and continued shooting until the sun set.

I counted the hours I practiced and realized I was shooting for about four hours.

How could Larry Bird practice six hours? Maybe he didn't eat dinner? No, he had to eat. Maybe he practiced more on Saturdays when he didn't have to go to school and it averaged out to be six hours a day for the week? For that to be true he would need to practice sixteen hours on a Saturday. Maybe he practiced six hours a day during the summer when he didn't have school? However he did it, he practiced every available minute he had so that's what I'm going to do; practice every available minute.

Every day after school I would begin shooting layups from just a few feet away on both sides of the basket, left to right, aiming to hit the high corner of the square on the backboard which would bank the layup shot off the backboard and in through the net. Next I would shoot jump shots in multiples of five or ten consecutive attempts from a spot along the baseline, moving to a diagonal spot, onto a middle spot facing the backboard and continuing to rotate around from baseline, diagonal, middle, diagonal and completing the rotation on to the opposite side baseline. I would then expand out shooting from short to medium and long ranges of rotating semi-circles. Thirdly I would shoot free throws from the foul line usually in multiples of ten shots in a row at a time. Lastly, I would shoot from any spot on the court usually trying to make a certain number in a row like three or five before moving onto another random spot while always chasing down and rebounding my missed shots.

    I kept shooting each afternoon and Saturday, week after week like this for about three to four hours total each time; only taking a break to eat dinner. As autumn continued into winter, daylight became shorter but I didn't let the darkness or the cold stop me. I kept shooting long after the sun would set using the outdoor lights from the carport of my family and the garage of the Westenskows to still see. The colder the weather became, the more layers of clothing I wore and the tougher it became to shoot but still I kept shooting. When the snow came I kept shooting, even with the driveway covered in snow and little ice sickles clinging to the net of the basket, I kept shooting. I could barely get a grip on the ball with those thick puffy snow gloves on my hands and the ball would barely bounce on the snow covered pavement without me having to thrust or slam the ball down to get enough return bounce, but still I kept shooting. During the winter the sun set at about 4:30 or 5 at night so I kept shooting in the dark until around 7 with my gloves and coat on. Although I did my best to practice as long as possible, I averaged closer to two or three hours of shooting a day during the winter since it did become so cold.

I practiced shooting so much that the Westenskows had to keep replacing the net of their basket multiple times since it kept breaking apart.

CHAPTER 6

KEEP PRAYING

Angel: "Tim, why didn't you try out for the high school team?"

Me: "I did try out."

Angel: "And you didn't make it?"

To be continued...

Fast forward nine years to 1997, I am now eighteen years old, six-feet three-inches tall, weighing about 175 pounds, in twelfth grade as a senior attending American Fork High School.

I achieved two of the most inspired basketball performances in basketball history at the team tryouts in early November of 1997. Inspired because of the comeback, —coming back yet again after so many years of getting knocked down. True greatness is in those who come back.

Just come back.

Three major reasons stacked the odds against me from previously making the basketball teams from seventh through eleventh grades so far.

One, I had really bad knees which required major knee surgeries and I will talk about later.

Two, I went to five different schools in six years so the coaches didn't know me.

Three, politics in basketball existed sometimes at the schools I attended.

Since politics existed if you wanted to make the team you must basically dominate from beginning to end to give yourself a chance to break through the political walls built around you. If you want to break through, you can't just play equally good or even better than those already on the team, instead you must perform at record-breaking levels. And when you reach high school there are probably only between one to three spots actually available to make on a team since the majority are already filled with the players returning from the previous year.

After so much heartbreak year after year, I prepared to return in a big way by making the ultimate comeback. Even with my knees giving me so much pain and so many problems, I still pushed through to train harder than ever before in preparation for what would be my last tryout before I would graduate high school.

My training consisted of a combination of running one mile every morning to an outdoor basketball court at an elementary school to practice shooting, ball handling, passing, my defensive stance and running the return mile back home. Riding my bike every other day seven miles to the weight room, lifting weights and riding my bike the return seven mile trip back home. Doing plyometric jumping and conditioning exercises on the concrete stairs and sidewalks outside our house every other day and alternating each day between weightlifting and plyometrics. Resting on Sunday and praying a lot throughout each day.

My shooting sessions during the summer or after school in the fall consisted of me shooting between 300 to 500 shots which took between two to four hours about to complete each time. During the winter and spring of 1997 my sessions were longer, consisting of me shooting at least 1,000 shots on an outdoor court at night which took a little over four hours. When the summer came I shot less because I needed to devote more time to improving my physical conditioning to somehow find a way to overcome the problems and pain of my knees. When my knees felt good and functioned correctly I was always able to play basketball at unbeatable levels. When my knees hurt, I sometimes couldn't even play because on top of the pain, my knees simply wouldn't bend, extend or support the movements of my body properly.

I introduced myself to the head coach during the first week of school, explaining that I was new to this high school and asked him what dates the tryouts would be held. He asked me what high school I played basketball at before? Hesitantly I responded that I have not been able to make the team yet and asked him not to let that fact affect his judgement when he sees me play.

Often times when you are on the verge of victory, the dark side will put discouragement and frustration in your path in an attempt to stop you, so when weird or strange things happen to you this is usually evidence that you are on the right path or else you would not be experiencing so much opposition.

Suddenly, in addition to the problems and pain my knees were constantly giving me, I could barely even walk only days right before the tryouts. I went to my chiropractor and found out my hips were misaligned. My hip joint on one side was significantly higher than the other side causing a lot of friction from where the ball of my thigh bone or femur connected into the socket of the hip joint. Fortunately my chiropractor healed me at the last moment. What are the chances that something like this causing me to barely even walk would happen just days before the tryouts? I knew what was going on, I knew the dark side was again attempting to stop me so I took courage that victory must be close at hand.

I asked my dad to give me a priesthood blessing the night before the tryouts would begin so that my knees would be healed. In the blessing my dad said Heavenly Father was very pleased with me and knew how hard I worked and that He would be with me and my knees would feel no pain and give me no problems during the tryouts.

After giving me the blessing, my dad and me hugged each other and he told me how happy and proud he was of me. Also my dad gave my sister, Polly, a blessing too since she was going to try out for the girls tenth grade basketball team.

Extremely nervous throughout the day is how I felt leading up to the starting hour of the tryouts that would begin after school. I was nervous not necessarily because I was scared but because my readiness was at its peak. I was ready to go. I was ready to play. I was ready to break some records and make history. The fire was building up inside me and it takes peak focus to maintain peak energy levels before unleashing it prematurely. Every hour, every minute, every second, I visualized in my mind my plan of how I was going to execute my comeback. I visualized every shot, every move, every pass, every box out, every rebound, every screen, every run up the floor, every run down the floor, every steal, every blocked shot, every defensive stop, every cheer and support to a teammate over and over and over in my mind. I visualized myself giving unstoppable effort and energy never before seen or experienced by anyone.

As I was stretching and warming up with that constant nervous feeling eating away at my stomach, I noticed how great my knees felt. Miraculously my knees were giving me absolutely no pain and no problems. I couldn't remember a time in years when my knees felt this good.

God is close by.

As soon as the ball was tipped at mid-court to start the first scrimmage, all my nervousness instantly vanished and I became extremely calm and relaxed.

Unleash the fire...

My first shot was a three-pointer that hit nothing but air, falling well short of the hoop. My next shot was a determined drive along the baseline finishing in a perfect reverse layup except for one thing; my layup was another airball even though I released the ball only inches away from the basket.

My first two shot attempts were airballs. Nothing but air. Not exactly how I visualized starting off the game and the tryouts.

But did I become discouraged after badly missing both shots? No, not for a moment. I actually took courage knowing I was on the verge of victory because my effort was there and as long as I kept giving my best effort I knew the results would eventually follow through.

Nothing and nobody can stop you from doing your best. Nothing and nobody can stop you from being unstoppable except yourself.

I took the point of view that this is a test I can choose to pass or fail. I have the power. I can choose to shrink or choose to shine. I chose to turn a negative situation into a positive situation by embracing the time to shine. ...This is it!

I could hear the oohs and aahs from my teammates, the opposing players and those standing around the gym and sitting in the bleachers. I was making shot after shot, making so many and creating so many plays that I turned the scrimmage into a display of pure victory. You know when you hear even your opponents saying "ooh", "aah", or "wow" under their breath and cheering you on that you have triumphed and made basketball history.

We won the scrimmage in a blowout.

We played two, 20-minute halves with a running clock, meaning the clock would keep running through every pause in play such as free throws and foul calls by the referees. A little over 40 players were trying out, divided into teams of five players on each. Our scrimmage started off the tryouts being that our game was the first of the afternoon. I came in and out like a whirlwind. All eyes were on me.

On my walk home, I replayed the game in my mind, adding up all the shots I made. I scored 25 points. I held the player I personally defended to 0 points. As best I could remember our team scored 37. The score was definitely in the upper 30's and I believe it was 37 since I scored twice as many points than the rest of our team combined. The exact score of the opposing team I can't remember either but it was in the upper teens for sure and I believe it was 18 since our team scored about twice as many points than our opponents. In summary, we won with probably an accurate but still an estimated score of 37-18 with me scoring 25 points and holding my man scoreless on the night.

At the end of the first half there was a play where I caught the pass on the left diagonal-wing outside the three-point line, faked a three-point shot which put my defender to sleep for that split second allowing me to drive to my left and straight past him along the baseline and towards the basket. Upon reaching the lane two more defenders emerged to create a wall between me and the hoop. Since I was now triple teamed, I abruptly dribbled back out acting like I was going to dribble all the way out but swiftly I spun back around surprising my three defenders who were mentally sleeping for that fraction of a second, thinking they had stopped me. As soon as I spun around the first defender, I then drove straight past the second defender and floated a nice little high-arcing drop shot over the outstretched arms of the last defender, swishing the ball through the net just seconds before the halftime buzzer sounded. The sounds of the oohs and aahs were prevalent among the surrounding players; teammates, opponents and bystanders alike.

In basketball and in life, just keep moving. Even when you are tired and can barely move, just move what you can. Do not stop. Finish the race.

Keep moving.
Keep helping.
Keep a positive attitude.
Keep having fun.
Keep winning.

Keep moving:
The person or team that keeps moving wins! Continuous effort or movement wears down all opposition, breaks down all obstacles, overcomes all negatives. Continuous effort or movement triumphs!

Keep helping:
The person or team that keeps helping wins! The person or team that keeps following the Golden Rule wins!

Three basic fundamental helping skills, out of a countless number, that I will highlight now are: setting screens, passing and communicating.

To some, setting screens may seem boring since it is not flashy like making an amazing shot but if the goal is to win and to be a winner then in actuality there is nothing more exciting than helping your team by settings screens.

For those who don't know, a "screen," or a "pick" as it is also called, is when you become a human wall to screen or pick off the path of an opposing player causing that opponent to move around your wall which creates space for your teammate to break free and get open. If the defender tries to push through your stationary wall rather than go around it, then this is a foul.

Setting screens for my teammates is one of my favorite things to do because it gets everyone moving, involved, feeling good and having fun. I love to set cross screens, down screens, up screens, back screens, side screens, curl screens, ball screens, screens away from the ball, fake screens, any screen you can imagine or invent; have fun with it and get creative!

One example of a screen would be a cross screen. I position myself a few feet away from the basket on either the left or right side of the lane, cross the lane to reach the opposite side where my teammate currently is positioned and set a pick on the opponent guarding my teammate which allows my teammate to break free. Now my newly freed teammate is open to receive a pass near the basket for a shot that has a high probability of going through the hoop.

Or other times, after helping your teammate get open with a pick, the opposition will become distracted and forget about you who just set the screen and direct attention toward your teammate, leaving you open instead for a high-percentage shot. Screens will get your teammate open, you open, or both at the same time depending on how, where and when you position and time your movements. Keep setting screens and you will keep wearing down the opposition not just physically but mentally.

Performing fake screens will also get you open by acting like you are going to set a screen, but then a split second before establishing your human wall, you instead free yourself by running or cutting in an unexpected direction.

The games that are the most fun are the ones when multiple teammates are simultaneously helping each other by getting creative with setting screens in all sorts of different directions, angles, spots and places. Have fun with it.

Who can I help?

The first thought on my mind each time I run up the floor on offense without the ball in my hands is: "who can I set a screen for?" And when the ball is in my hands, my first thought is: "who can I pass to?"

Continuous screening and passing creates continuous movement, free and open spaces, good shots, opportunities, rhythm, dancing, and fun for everyone. I love and appreciate when someone sets a screen for me or passes me the ball so I want to do the same for my teammates. When someone helps me, I can see that this person is a winner and if I also want to be a winner myself I need to help others too.

I scored the majority of the points during this first game of the tryouts not because I was selfish but because I kept helping. Because I kept passing and setting screens I was able to find open spaces, pathways, spots, and lanes where the ball would find its way back to me for good shots. The ball will find its way to one of your teammates or back to you and either way, whether your teammate makes the shot or you individually make the shot, it doesn't matter who scores the points, what matters is that the team scores as a result of helping each other. And points are scored not just from making shots on offense but also from stopping your opponents from making shots on defense and the easiest way to defend is simply by helping each other.

The person or team that keeps communicating or cheering each other on wins! Letting your teammates and even your opponents know that you care about and value them is a divine quality.

Besides cheering on my teammates by letting them know the good and positive things I see each one of them doing, I also cheer on my opponents. At this tryout, I perceived one opposing player was becoming discouraged during the game so I cheered him on and encouraged him to keep going and not give up.

This is basketball and basketball is about helping each other.

Keep a positive attitude:

The person or team that keeps turning negative situations into positive situations simply by changing the movement of their thoughts wins!

Nothing can stop you from thinking positively except yourself. Positive thinking creates positive action which produces the positive result of winning. No good thing has ever come from negative thinking.

Darkness cannot bring light. Look for and see the positive in even the most negative of situations and you can never lose, can never be defeated, you will always win and be forever undefeated.

Keep having fun:
    The person or team that keeps having fun wins! If you're not having fun, you're doing something wrong. If you're not having fun, you're either not moving, not helping or not thinking positively.

Keep winning:
    When everyone is moving, helping by including and involving one another, feeling good or positive, and having fun is when victory appears. Move, move move, help, help, help, stay positive and have fun! That is basketball.

    Our team won easily again on the second night of the tryouts.
    We were again the first game of the evening and this time I was matched-up to guard one of the star players who was physically much larger than me, reaching a height of almost seven feet. Another player told me this star player was a basketball phenomenon.
    Basketball and life is not about who is the biggest, fastest or strongest, it is about the effort or the

movement, helping, staying positive and having fun; it is about doing your best which overcomes all obstacles. It is about doing the things you have complete control over. The thing you always have complete control over is your effort.

You do not have only some control over your effort. On the contrary, you have total control over your effort. You can always keep coming back, you can always get back up.

The teams were changed from yesterday and again the head coach decided the match-ups just like he did last night, he decided who would guard who so he could get a better look at the strengths and weaknesses of each player.

I scored 8 points this time, making 4 shots out of 6 attempts, and held my man to 4 points. Being that he was much larger than me and one of the star players, his team ran a lot of plays specifically for him and kept feeding him the ball repeatedly.

UCLA basketball coach John Wooden taught that basketball is a game of position, timing and skills or in other words it is a game of effort.

Your effort controls or decides where you go which is "position", when you go which is "timing" and how you go or move which is "skills".

The more you practice, the more you keep moving, the more you keep giving your best effort then the more you improve, refine, polish and perfect your position, timing and skills.

Your heart and mind control your effort. If you

believe in your mind or heart you cannot win then you will lose. If you believe in your mind or heart you can win then you will win. No matter what a situation might appear like, no matter how dire, dark, or impossible, appearances can be deceiving but your effort can never be deceived; give your best effort and all deceiving appearances will disappear.

So even though the player I was guarding was much taller and bigger than me, a couple specific effort-things I did to make it difficult for him to score was positioning myself lower than himself in a defensive stance to leverage away his strength and size so he could not push his way close to the basket, and positioning myself to get in front of the passing lanes at the right times to deny him from receiving the basketball near the hoop.

When I was on offense the opposing team was so concerned about me going off on another scoring explosion like I did last night that the defense frequently made attempts at double teaming me. The specific defensive planning and attention paid to me opened everything up for my teammates to get free for good shots making it easy for us to win again.

Just like last night, as soon as the ball was tipped at mid-court all of my nervousness instantly disappeared.

Anticipating some players might try to convince themselves my performance last night was a fluke, I used their mentality to my advantage as I casually positioned myself out of sight along the baseline, mentally putting my opponents to sleep. While they were mentally napping I saw an opportunity developing to shoot from the corner of the free throw line which is also called the elbow and is one of my favorite spots to shoot from. When the ball reached my teammate at the top of the key outside the three-point line I aggressively sprinted up to another teammate hanging around the free throw line and tightly curled around his body from right to left, using him as a screen to rub off my opponent and break free for a split second to shoot. My teammate that I curled around was not trying to set a screen for me, he was just standing there but instead of waiting for help to come to me, I went and found help. Before completing the full curl I called out for the ball, then caught the pass, finished curling, squared my feet and shoulders to face the basket on the left side elbow of the free throw line, and then focused keeping my elbow straight and aligned with the hoop as I raised up into the air to take my first shot. Knocking the ball loose from my hands as I reached the peak of my jump, my almost seven-foot-tall opponent appeared to have successfully blocked my shot.

 Yet, as I simultaneously descended from my peak, I countered in midair by resetting my hands to regain control of the ball and shoot again with a fadeaway release of the ball just inches before I landed. The acrobatic, two-shots-in-one jump shot sweetly swished through the hoop for my first two points of the game. Astounded expressions appeared on the faces of my opponent and others. Backpedaling back down the court I looked over to my left directly at the head coach, sitting in the bleachers at his table taking notes, to make sure he was paying attention and to let him know my message. He was indeed paying attention and as we made eye contact I let him know the message is: I'm back again.

When I woke up the following morning I was so nervous I felt like I was going to throw up all day long. I couldn't eat anything. Anytime I smelled food I felt very nauseated. At lunch, I got my pasta, sat down, put the fork stuck with curly noodles up to my mouth and felt like throwing up. Today was the day to find out if I made the cuts.

Here we go again.

So many times before when I tried out and had a great performance I thought the coaches had seen it and saw me and I was going to make the cut for sure. And so many times I failed to make it and was left to wonder; what is going on? Am I crazy or something? Are the coaches that blind?

Here I was this time after giving two back-to-back brilliant and inspired performances and I was worried that I was about to enter the Twilight Zone again.

My heart was bursting out of my chest, I could hardly breathe as I approached the main doors of the gym where the list of names of those who made the cuts were posted. I didn't want to look. I quietly said a prayer in my heart and asked Heavenly Father to help me not to be afraid and that no matter what happens "I know You have been helping me."

    I slowly started reading the names from the top down...

    ...Tim McGaffin.

    I'm back again.

    I felt as if the prison walls around me were falling away. I felt restored. I said a little thank you prayer in my heart.

    A little over 40 players to start the tryout transitioned to about 20 players with 15 spots to make on the team, consisting of a combination of two teams; both the junior varsity and varsity teams combined into one team of 15 players.

    The hour to start the tryouts on this third day approached. Just like the prior two nights, as soon as the ball was tipped at mid-court to start the game that nauseated feeling eating away at me instantly vanished.

    Unlike the first two days however, I struggled tonight. I struggled because I had absolutely no energy. I was running on fumes. I had not been able to eat a single thing all day. Actually, even the first two days of tryouts I was able to eat very little. Mainly I was able to eat only dinner the first two days, feeling too nervous to eat much of anything for breakfast or lunch. This lack of being able to eat and constantly feeling like throwing up for the last three days caught up to me. I prayed a lot throughout each day asking God to help me not feel nervous like this. I know He heard my prayers but yet the nervousness wouldn't go away until I was actually on the court playing. Although, He did heal my knees for these tryouts, I didn't understand why God wouldn't also take away my nervousness except that He works in mysterious and victorious ways.

One of the assistant coaches came up to me after the game tonight to talk to me in private. He told me not to worry about my performance. He said, "you've had an impressive tryout so far" and that if I come back tomorrow with a solid performance I will probably make the team. He asked me where I came from and what high schools I played at before? I answered that I have not made my school teams for five consecutive years now.

On this fourth and final night of the tryouts as soon as the ball was tipped at mid-court all my nervousness again immediately retreated.

It all came down to this, my fourth and final match-up of the tryout. I believe the head coach beforehand, planned to pick the player who would play better overall between us both in this match-up, as to which one of us would be picked to make the team.

I saw the opposing screen coming. I knew exactly what play was being ran. I knew my man was going to do a back-door cut behind me diagonally towards the basket to try and get an easy shot but my body, still running on fumes with absolutely no energy, couldn't move as quickly as my mind was telling myself to move and my man was able to squeeze a catch and score on an easy shot just feet away from the basket.

My effort was extraordinary but my results were average this evening. Although the results didn't equal the effort I put forth this time, the effort this time will carry over to the next time and the results will eventually follow through.

I gave everything, everything I could possibly give mentally and spiritually and physically with all my heart, and stood there alone on the court exhausted ...and discouraged.

I was so close. I came in like a whirlwind on the first two nights and finished on this fourth night directing my thoughts heavenward.

"Dear Heavenly Father, I feel very frustrated and discouraged. You took the pain away from my knees. You were with me. I did my best but I feel discouraged. I need your help. Please help me to not feel this way. I know I did my very best, and I know that You know I did my very best."

A few days later the bishop of my ward (church congregation) whose name is Mont Beardall, and whose son, Danny, I became friends with since my family moved to American Fork in the spring, —gave me a ride home in his car after a church youth activity.

On the ride home, he revealed to me that he witnessed me play at the tryouts.

"Oh, ...you were there?", I said astonishingly.

I didn't know he was there, I didn't see him anywhere. He said he was up high in the bleachers where no one could see him.

I asked what days he was there. He said he was there the first two days.

I could tell simply by the expression on his face he really felt impressed with my performances and wanted me to know the truth.

"I really thought you ran the floor well," Bishop Beardall told me. He went on to explain that he thought I ran, kept moving, had better energy, and that I looked to be in better conditioning than anyone.

I was very excited and thankful that he saw that in me. I told him I had a goal to be the first one up the floor on offense and the first one down the floor on defense. I asked him if it looked like I accomplished that goal? He said that I did.

That is my secret weapon, I revealed; to keep moving, to never give up. I said to win in life and in basketball all we need to do is keep moving, to never quit no matter what. He enthusiastically agreed.

I told him I struggled the last two days and that was probably the reason why I wasn't picked to make the team. If I dominated all four days, and not just the first two, I probably would've finally made the team this time, I said.

Beardall said regardless of how I played the last two days, my first two performances alone proved I'm as good of a basketball player as the best high school players anywhere. Although some high school teams are more difficult to make than others and it is a very hard decision for coaches to make when choosing which players make the team, he said I proved myself regardless.

Finally, I told him that I'm not going to give up, I will tryout to make a team in college after I serve my two-year church mission. I will be back again. I know that God is helping me, and as long as I keep trusting in Him I know I will achieve my dream, I said. He encouraged me to not give up and said he believed in me and wholeheartedly agreed that with God helping us, all good things are accomplished.

Each time you do your very best, God is close by helping you. When God is close by helping you, you do the impossible. Don't try your best. Do your best! Do your best and you do the impossible every time with the help of God.

Remember, when the odds are stacked against you, as long as you are doing your best to overcome those odds, God is close by your side helping you even if it sometimes may appear He is not there.

The coaches didn't know me because they hadn't seen me play before these tryouts. I had no references in the form of other high school coaches to put in a good word for me either since I hadn't made those school teams for the previous five years. As well, me not making those teams so far could indicate falsely that I'm not qualified to play basketball on the high school level and could cause subjective judgement or cloudy vision, before even seeing me play.

Also on the first day the head coach announced he would pick younger players, such as a junior or sophomore, over a senior —even if the senior played better— so he could have an extra year or two to work on developing the potential of the younger player if he felt their potential would equal or surpass the current senior in the future. And the only seniors who made the team this year were all returning from the team the year before.

In general, the returning players from the team the year before didn't face the same odds as I did in this tryout situation because our performances were measured by unequal standards.

For example, the returning team players could perform equal to or even slightly less than everyone else and they would most likely make the team again, as they should, because they already proved themselves previously in other games outside of this tryout.

Being that I was the unknown, I would instead be required every day to play, not just better, but significantly better than all the returning players to prove myself and break through onto the team. If I played slightly less than the returning players, the odds were not in my favor to be picked to make the team over the current players. If I played equal to or even better than the returning players, the odds were still not in my favor to be picked because the coaches would most likely need to cut one of the current team players to make room for me. Therefore, in order to make it easier to justify replacing one of the current team players with the previously unknown player, I would need to perform significantly better than the current team players every day of the tryouts as to leave no doubts whatsoever in the minds of the coaches that they were indeed making the right choice.

And to quickly illustrate how rare it really is to dominate four nights in a row I will use scoring as an example. The best NBA players are capable of scoring two-thirds of the total points of their entire teams. However, even though they're capable of scoring record amounts, they only score those levels on rare occasions.

With all these factors understood, it's a difficult decision for the coaches to make and it's a difficult situation for me to be in. Yet, the absolute most difficult situation to be in, is when you get knocked down...

...and then come back!

I fully desired, believed, prepared, and planned to dominate all four nights in a row with the help of God; and I did achieve the impossible all four nights in a row just by coming back.

You overcome all the odds and achieve the impossible when you come back whether the world sees your victory or not.

Nothing can stop me or you from overcoming the impossible every time since nothing can stop us from doing our best every time except ourselves.

The very fact that the odds have stacked against you when you are getting back up does not mean God is not there but rather is proof that God is there and that you are on the very verge of the triumph! There is so much opposition sometimes when you are doing your best because the dark side knows who you are, knows you are a child of God, and knows how near you are to the triumph; and consequently will throw everything it has at you at the last minute in an attempt to discourage and deceive you into falsely thinking that either God is not there or that you cannot come back (overcome the odds) or both. If you let yourself be deceived into thinking either one of these false scenarios then you will stop yourself since you are the only one who can stop you.

No matter what a situation may appear to be, just do your best and know God will be close by your side. God really will be close by you, not in some imaginary sense, He really will be there. Just hold on a little longer...

A number of weeks later on a Saturday morning in late January of 1998, I scored 36 points before severely spraining my right ankle with about two minutes left in the game. We won the game. A lot of our points came from pick-and-roll or screen-and-roll plays of teamwork. Because of this injury, this game became the last one in which I played, in the regular season of the local church basketball league.

At the hospital, before an X-ray was taken, the doctor initially thought I broke my foot upon viewing my ankle swelling to the size of a large ruby red grapefruit.

Earlier in this same month of January in another Saturday morning church game we won, I remember scoring about 11 points and after the game the head referee approached me with a question:

"Tim, why didn't you try out for the high school team?"

"I did try out," I answered.

"And you didn't make it?", he asked in shock.

I explained I played really well the first two days of tryouts but because I was so nervous I couldn't eat anything so I had no energy and I didn't play as well the last two days.

"Well, I'm going to need to have a talk with Coach _____ and ask him why he didn't put you on the team," he said. "You should be on the team."

With a thankful heart that this referee could see me, I asked him if he was friends with the head coach or if he knew him well?

He replied:

"I was the coach before Coach _____."

I sincerely thanked him for letting me know, essentially, that he could see me. To me, he was an angel who had been sent to give me a message Heavenly Father wanted me to know.

He really helped me a lot.

He was a prior head coach of the American Fork High School basketball team.

He thought the reason why I must not be on the team was simply because I must not have chosen to show up and try out. Upon discovering that I did try out and still didn't make the team, he seemed amazed in disbelief.

He was always kind to me each game. While refereeing he would point out to me the things he saw me doing well. For example he recognized my skill for positioning and timing myself in setting screens and getting my teammates open. He saw my skill for positioning and timing to get rebounds; timing to get rebounds by seeing missed shots before they missed by identifying where the ball, after being shot and still in midair, would most likely bounce off the rim and in what direction the ball would most likely fly through the air and then timing to consistently grab those missed shots.

Also my knees during these organized church basketball games were really hurting me again. After the tryouts the pain and problems of my knees returned. Still, even with my knees giving me problems again, he saw me.

I could tell he knew what basketball was about because he could see the effort as a tangible thing.

My original plan was to make the high school team, practice and improve my skills to become one of the best players on the team, garner the attention of some colleges or universities, be recruited to probably play at a two-year school like a junior college or community college and then transfer to a four-year Division 1 college team. Then finally after college I could concentrate on making it to the NBA.

Being now that I didn't make the team in my final year of high school it again sometimes seemed or appeared God was not with me. I knew God was with me but even though I knew, it was still hard not to have doubts and feel frustrated or discouraged at times.

When he told me I should be on the team and finding out he used to be the basketball coach I felt restored once again from receiving another witness confirming to me God really is there with me and really is helping me no matter what the situation falsely appears to be.

Twelve months later in January 1999, I was days away from leaving to serve a mission for two years to Lisbon, Portugal for The Church of Jesus Christ of Latter-Day Saints.

Before I left I was going through the temple for my first time at the Mount Timpanogos Temple on Friday January 22.

Herschel Pederson, who served in the temple, met with me and my parents and asked me:

"Do you believe God answers your prayers?"

I said that I absolutely believe and know God answers my prayers.

Pederson then asked me to read a scripture in The Book of Mormon. The scripture was 2 Nephi, chapter 32, verse 9:

"But behold, I say unto you that ye must pray always, and not faint; that ye must not perform any thing unto the Lord save in the first place ye shall pray unto the Father in the name of Christ, that he will consecrate thy performance unto thee, that thy performance may be for the welfare of thy soul."

After I finished reading the scripture out loud, Pederson counseled me that I should pray and ask God for two specific dreams to come true. One of the two dreams I should pray for is what I should do in my life. Whatever I wanted to do in my life, I should write it down and pray in my personal prayers every day asking God to help me; and that God will make my dream come true.

Pederson then gave the example of his son who wanted to be a medical doctor. His son prayed and asked God to help him and he did become a doctor and his son knew it was because the Lord was the one who helped him make his dream come true.

I had never met Herschel Pederson before, I had no idea who he was, I had never spoken one word to him but here he was giving me a message directly from Heaven, a message only God could have inspired him to reveal to me.

Only my parents, Mama and Poppy, my brother and sister, Patrick and Polly, and God knew that I prayed when I was little asking for help to know what I should do when I grow up and to make that dream come true.

Again Heavenly Father was speaking to me, letting me know He is there. He has always been there from the very beginning. And He will always continue to be there until my dream comes true.

As it says in this scripture 2 Nephi 32:9, a prayer is a "performance" and a "performance" is a prayer. Our actions of faith are prayers.

Actions of faith are spiritual or physical or both.

When you communicate to God in your heart, or in your mind through your thoughts, or out loud through spoken thoughts which are words: That's a prayer.

As well, when you physically follow your heart, or act on your thoughts or act on your words: That's a prayer.

If one of the desires of my heart is to be the greatest basketball player ever then I need to do. I need to act. I need to do whatever I possibly can that is within my control and God will "consecrate" my "performance" so that I will receive my dream as long as what I desire is good and right; that what I desire is for the "welfare of my soul".

For example, every time I practice: that's a prayer. Every time I practice improving specific skills such as ball handling, passing, shooting, setting screens, defense or any skill: that's a prayer.

Each time I go training: that's a prayer. Each time I go running: that's a prayer. Each time I go running and feel almost exhausted and I still keep going until I pass the next tree, the next street corner, the next sign, the next fence: that's a prayer. Each time I go to the weight room and lift weights: that's a prayer. Each time I eat right, sleep right, read a good book, turn negative thoughts into positive thoughts, treat others right: that's a prayer.

Later I went back and read the previous verse. I read verse 8 of chapter 32 of 2 Nephi where it says:

> "For if ye would hearken unto the Spirit which teacheth a man to pray ye would know that ye must pray; for the evil spirit teacheth not a man to pray, but teacheth him that he must not pray."

Never believe the lies or illusions of the dark side. God is there and will help you if you so desire.

Keep moving.
Keep helping.
Keep a positive attitude.
Keep having fun.
Keep winning.

...Keep praying.

CHAPTER 7

NEVER NEVER GIVE UP!

Champions reveal themselves not during the easy times but during the difficult times.

During the difficult times the still small voice of God is always there telling each of us: "Don't give up."

The message of "never give up" and "never quit" is constantly being communicated to each of us everywhere we look. The key is to actually look in order to see the message. If you don't look, if you don't exercise faith then you will not clearly see.

The message is always there, communicating to each of us through the word of God in the holy scriptures, good books, uplifting music, art, and film; being communicated through our talents and other champions.

God gives each of us divine gifts and talents to fulfill divine purposes. One way God reveals Himself is through our gifts and talents when we share them and go after our dreams.

I turned eight years old on August 23, 1987 and in September, after coming home from school in the late afternoon, there was an entertainment news program on television. Michael Jackson appeared at the end of the show in his short film for his new song called "Bad".

This is the first time in my life I saw and heard Michael Jackson perform.

Immediately I recognized he sang with all his heart and soul. Seeing this got me really excited. Secondly, I immediately saw he always kept moving; he always kept dancing, dancing, dancing.

After watching Michael Jackson sing and dance with all his heart and soul for less than 30 seconds, I said out loud to myself: "He is the best. He is the best ever!"

I also remember thinking that I'm only eight years old and have only seen and heard a small amount of songs from other musicians and I know the adults won't believe me since I'm little but I don't need to see any more to already recognize and know that he is the best ever.

It was greatness at first sight.

Michael Jackson has profoundly inspired me countless times throughout my life to not give up. He has helped me so much to keep going after my dreams. If I wrote down all the times he has profoundly motivated me it would fill an entire book.

I've had multiple life-changing experiences listening to him sing with real heartfelt emotion and watching him dance with masterful precision and timing. He is a true king and a true champion. Michael inspires me to also be the best, to also be a king and champion like he is.

When asked what the message of his song "Unbreakable" is in a 2001 interview with TV Guide, Michael Jackson responded with the following: "That I'm invincible, that I've been through it all. You can't hurt me. Knock me down, I get back up."

One of the greatest and most profound experiences ever of my life was and always will be seeing and hearing Michael perform his song "Heal the World" live in concert. Seeing all of the people in the crowd and all of the children onstage singing and uniting together to "Heal the World" forever uplifts my heart to look to and focus on God no matter how discouraging or frustrating things become because with the help of God the true triumph will ultimately come.

In listening to the songs Michael wrote and composed, obstacles always appear within his music represented by the moments of tension. That tension or those obstacles are always overcome by the continuously moving and unstoppable rhythm, beat and melody.

In watching Michael interpret and express the music in his live performances, the obstacles are always overcome by his dancing and energy because he keeps going, he keeps moving, he never stops, he never gives up until the triumph.

In October my family, the McGaffin Five, was

able to go on vacation to Disneyland in Anaheim, California thanks to Uncle Jim and Tom Gable from Columbia, Pennsylvania who gave my parents some funds to help pay for the trip because Uncle Jim and Uncle Tom wanted us to go. The main attraction for me was seeing Captain EO, Michael Jackson's 17-minute short film in 3D. Captain EO was one of the most inspiring things I have ever felt. I remember Michael floating on air, gliding and hovering when he danced, the greatest dancing ever. The message and music of the film really inspired me. Shine your light with the help of God and all darkness will disappear and be replaced with the beauty and goodness of the light and truth.

On Christmas Day of this same year of 1987, Santa Claus gave me Michael Jackson's Bad album and this is the day when I watched Star Wars for the first time in my life.

Star Wars, the film by George Lucas, was on television Christmas night. The main thing I kept thinking to myself as I watched the film is that Darth Vader, the villain, is unstoppable.

Or at least, he seemed to be unstoppable.

Upon closer inspection I learned Darth Vader was not truly unstoppable; it was all an illusion.

Darth Vader let himself be seduced by the dark side and made the choice to become evil because he stopped looking to God and then gave up when times got really tough.

When the hard times came, Vader gave into his

fear, he turned away from God and his fear turned into hate. The most evil people are really the most scared, they pretend to not be scared of anything but they are the most frightened of all.

The dark side wants to convince us through deceit, lies, fraud, cheating, that evil cannot be stopped but the truth is the other way around. The truth is that evil is afraid of champions because evil knows champions truly are the ones that cannot be stopped. This is why the dark side is constantly attacking champions and truth to discourage others from awakening and arising. Evil knows once you awake and arise to the light, once you make the choice, once you make the commitment that you will never never never give up; then there is nothing that can stop you!

In choosing to do what is right in those difficult times is when the miracle is revealed, when the light shines on the darkness and the darkness comprehendeth it not, and when the champion is revealed.

> "We need not become paralyzed with fear of Satan's power. He can have no power over us unless we permit it. [Satan] is really a coward, and if we stand firm, he will retreat."
> –James E. Faust[1]

Before Darth Vader turned to evil he worked hard to choose the right. However, when the difficult

---

1. *The Great Imitator, General Conference October 1987; The Forces That Will Save Us, Ensign January 2007*

times came, instead of turning to God to give him the true power to keep going, Vader instead turned to the dark side. Many times previously Vader chose good but it seemed the results of his right choices frequently brought failure and pain.

When bad things happen to good people, the darkness is there to tempt you to believe its lies by saying something like this: "See, God doesn't care about you. Why didn't God stop this pain and suffering from happening to you?"

Darth Vader chose to turn away from the light and toward the false promises of unlimited power because he wanted to overcome and eliminate all obstacles, failure and pain.

The truth is the power of the dark side is limited, it is temporary because darkness always comes to an end.

In choosing the right, in making the commitment to be a champion, there will be times where you will be slowed down but those difficult, painful, dark times are limited, temporary and they will all come to an end because there is no end to light; there is only the triumph!

Later in Star Wars, Obi-Wan Kenobi, who is on the good side meets Darth Vader in a futuristic duel with swords of light called lightsabers.

Kenobi has been through similar painful times that Vader has been through. They grew up together, were friends, fought side by side in the Clone Wars years earlier. Yet despite experiencing similar hard times, Kenobi continued to follow the light because, unlike Vader, Kenobi never gave up.

During the lightsaber duel between Darth Vader and Obi-Wan Kenobi, between good and evil, Kenobi says:

"You can't win Darth. If you strike me down I shall become more powerful than you can possibly imagine."

Kenobi, facing his possible looming death at the hands of evil, reveals himself during this difficult time by courageously shining his light to let Vader know there is more than meets the physical mortal eye.

Star Wars and the subsequent five films is based on history and tells the true story of good versus evil. The storytelling talents of George Lucas and his artistic teammates reminds me many times the difference between good and evil and to choose the good no matter what.

The best source to study and learn about the differences between good and evil is from the holy scriptures that contain the word and voice of God. Star Wars and the artistry of these six films, does well in bringing multiple true principles contained in the scriptures and found in history, to life.

The sixth Star Wars film, Revenge of the Sith, expertly shows the true and actual patterns, methods, and techniques Satan or evil implements every time to take over governments, and seduce, deceive and convince others to wrongly choose evil over good.

Also in this same twelve-month period after

turning eight years old from August of 1987 to August of 1988 is when I also saw John Stockton, Karl Malone and their Utah Jazz teammates play basketball for the first time in my life.

As I wrote earlier, I learned a lot about true winning, about coming back again and again and again, about continuing to move forward when you are down from watching Stockton and Malone and other Jazz teammates play basketball. The dream of John and Karl was to win the NBA championship, —to be the best. They came so close to winning the championship so many times year after year after year. Each time they lost, they came right back the next year working harder and more determined, dedicated, and devoted than ever before to win that championship.

On June 2, 1998 the head coach of the Utah Jazz, Jerry Sloan, when speaking to the media about the NBA Finals, said: "A lot of people talk about winning a championship, and that's an amazing thing. But the more amazing thing is to lose and then come back and try to do it again, which our guys did. They put everything they could in to try and have a chance to win, and that takes a tremendous amount of concentration and desire to even get to that point again."

"It had been reported that we needed to get rid of Stockton and Malone because they were getting too old," Sloan continued. "And that's when they pushed up and made it to the Finals a couple of years in a row."

Stockton and Malone never gave up, they never

quit, they always came back. Each year they returned stronger than ever. Their examples really helped me to also keep moving forward no matter what the score appears to be and to keep returning to try out to make the team year after year after year just like Stockton and Malone.

God communicates to me to "hold on just a little longer" through champions like my mother, Kathleen; my father, Timothy John McGaffin, who I am named after; my sister Pollyanna and my brother Patrick.

Remember it was my parents who taught me, and my sister and brother, Polly and Pat, to pray and ask God for help with anything our hearts desired.

When Polly was six years old, she prayed for a cat and the next day Friskey appeared in our backyard.

When Roger —one of Friskey's sons— was very sick, Pat prayed that Roger wouldn't die and Roger lived an impossibly long time considering how sick he was and we know it was because of God.

As you recall, I started praying when I was about seven years old to specifically know what I should do and be in my life. I did not receive that specific answer to that specific daily prayer until September of 1988, shortly after my ninth birthday in August. Although I did not receive a specific answer for more than a year of daily prayers, I did receive answers during this time through the divine gifts and talents of Michael Jackson, George Lucas, John Stockton, and Karl Malone.

It is not a coincidence that I saw and felt the gifts

and talents of Jackson, Lucas, Stockton and Malone each for the first time in my life during the same time that I began to specifically pray daily to find out my dream.

Heavenly Father knew I wanted to be the best ever. He knew the difficulty of the journey that awaited me. He knew there would be many times I would feel discouraged. He knew I had a lot to learn about continuing to move forward during the most difficult of situations. It is not a coincidence then that God, in addition to my family, gave me more role models at the same time I started specifically praying to receive a specific answer for a specific dream. Role models who would continually uplift, inspire and motivate me to make that dream I was praying for come true. Role models who each look to God to help them each not to give up, to help them each make their dreams come true, to help them each become the best ever, to help them each become champions. Michael Jackson is the best singer, dancer, musician and live performer ever. George Lucas is the best storyteller through film ever. Stockton and Malone are the best basketball players ever. My mom is the best artist ever and my dad is also the best basketball player ever and I will talk about both later.

Anybody who looks to God to help them never give up is the best ever!

The world will not see the truth of who you are but God sees you and knows who you are because God looks on the heart and not the outward appearance.

Throughout my journey God inspires, uplifts and helps me by the divine gifts and talents, stories and journeys of other champions to be a champion myself. Who better to learn from and emulate than the best. I have been profoundly inspired by many heroes and their victories. If it was not for these truly great people God surrounded me with I would not have been able to make my dream that God gave me come true. I would not have been able to keep getting back up without their examples.

Shine your light. Recognize your God-given talents, cultivate and develop them, and then share them. Go after your dreams! When you feel inspired to do something, do it. Fulfill the divine purposes of your gifts and talents.

The greatest talent is doing what is right, seeking after light and truth and then following the light and living the truth; most simply, the greatest talent is "never giving up".

Recognizing truth is a talent. Seeing light is a talent. Going after your dreams is a talent. Listening is a talent. Learning is a talent. Asking questions is a talent. Reading is a talent. Caring is a talent. Service is a talent. Communicating is a talent. Sharing is a talent. Giving is a talent. Receiving is a talent. Helping is a talent. Forgiving is a talent. Believing is a talent. Praying is a talent. Exercising faith in God is a talent. All talents are spiritual or physical actions of doing what is right, of faith, of never giving up; multiple words that describe the same divine action.

Brainwashing is not a talent.

The dark side is the side of lies to brainwash or condition you to make you forget what your talents are and who you are. Degrading, uninspired, dark, and manipulative music, movies, television, advertising, and media lie to you. One specific example of brainwashing or propaganda that comes to mind are the attacks to break up the family.

Being a mother or a father and having children is a dream; a dream encompassing all of your talents.

The world or the dark side will try to falsely convince you that anybody can be a mother or a father and have children so it's nothing special. Saying falsely that being a mother or a father is nothing, that it's not important, that it's beneath you, it's not grandiose, it's boring, bland, and any other adjective you can think of that is the opposite of the truth. On the contrary, being married to the person of your dreams, motherhood, fatherhood and having a family is a heavenly dream given to you from God.

Also remember our time on earth is just one part of our journey, God is all-powerful so don't give up no matter what the situation may appear to be because all your dreams will come true. Shine your light! Never stop going after your dreams whether you are nine years old or one-hundred and nine years old.

When the difficult times come, "don't give up" and the miracle will be revealed in you; the victory will be revealed in you!

The message of "never give up" is all around us if we are looking for and listening to the voice of God. God is continually speaking and saying "don't give up" to each one of us personally.

"You have the worst knees I've ever seen," Dr. Kirt Kimball said.

I returned home on January 10, 2001 from serving as a missionary for two years in Lisbon, Portugal for The Church of Jesus Christ of Latter-Day Saints. I was now twenty-one years old.

Immediately I began implementing my carefully created training regimen in the mornings and evenings, while working part-time at Kentucky Fried Chicken in the afternoons, to get in shape to successfully tryout to make the basketball team this fall at Snow College; a two-year school in Ephraim, Utah.

Now is the time to make my planned comeback and reveal the victory.

There was one problem.

My knees were hurting me more than ever before.

I could walk but I could not run functionally correct because of the excruciating pain. The same pain I had off and on since I was thirteen years old. This time though, I could not even jump off one foot. And when standing on two feet I could barely jump more than a few inches. While standing on one foot I could lift my opposite thigh and knee into the air but could not extend the lower half of my leg out from below my knee; the lower half of my leg would just hang there vertically. When sitting down I could not extend out my legs from below either knee; my feet would only lift up slightly above the floor and my legs would shake as I tried to unsuccessfully extend my legs out horizontally.

Three visits to our regular family doctor, each time with my mom, and the doctor refused to take an X-ray of my knees. He thought the problem was tendinitis which is inflammation of the tendons and thought prescription drugs would solve the problem even though me and my mom kept saying we thought the problem was more serious than tendinitis. On the third visit to this doctor in a few weeks between February and March, after more repeated refusals to take an X-ray of my knees, my mom began yelling at the doctor: "We want an X-ray now!"

For whatever reason the doctor didn't want to X-ray my knees until my mom did what she felt inspired to do.

Upon viewing the X-rays, the doctor said, "Hmm, there is something wrong there."

He said he takes X-rays of hundreds of kids my age and sees no problems but with me he saw what could be a bone cyst or bone cancer.

He said he couldn't tell for sure what the problem was but whatever I had, it was in both knees and the chances were one in a million he said.

To determine exactly what the X-rays were

showing, I would need to be referred to see an orthopedic specialist.

My mom prayed and felt inspired we should see Dr. Kirt Kimball who is the orthopedic surgeon for Brigham Young University athletics. My mom found out there is usually a long waiting list for new patients to be able to see him. She called Kimball's office and was able to get me an appointment right away because Heavenly Father helped her she said.

We saw Dr. Kimball on Monday March 19, 2001 and immediately scheduled surgery for my right knee that Thursday.

Kimball looked at the previous X-rays from the family doctor and said, "this is not tendinitis." Then he took additional X-rays of both knees.

Dr. Kimball discovered I had the most severe case of a condition called osteochondritis dissecans in both my right and left knees.

Basically, I had huge pieces of bone that had broken away from both my right and left knees. Since there was no blood flow into the large disconnected fragments, those sections of bone died. The radiologist who took the X-rays told us he had never seen holes that large in knees of anyone else before.

Before my right knee surgery on March 22, 2001 my dad gave me a priesthood blessing that the doctors who would work on repairing my knee would be surprised at how well my knee is and that Heavenly Father wants me to achieve the desires of my heart and to remember to follow Him.

As I lay on the mobile hospital bed and the nurse preparing me for surgery, Dr. Kimball came to see me minutes before I was wheeled off for the operation and told the nurse and myself that I had the biggest holes in my knees of anyone he has worked on so far in his career.

"You have the worst knees I've ever seen," Dr. Kimball said to me.

When I awoke in the recovery room the nurse named Shauna saw me looking around and she came over and told me to keep the oxygen mask on and I said, "looks like I'll make that Jazz game."

We both started laughing because instead of me first asking about how the operation went, I expressed my excitement to be able to make it home in time to see the Utah Jazz play the Portland Trailblazers that evening on television.

When Dr. Kimball came by to see how I was doing he said he was surprised to see the cartilage was just fine, it wasn't in poor condition like he thought it would be. And instead of having to remove the broken fragments of dead bone he was able to attach those fragments to the living bone with three screws due to the surface of the living bone not being torn up either from where the large fragments broke off.

After Kimball left, I told my mom that he was "surprised" just like my dad blessed me would happen.

The surgery on my left knee occurred about six weeks later on May 1, 2001 and required two screws which were slightly larger than the three screws used for my right knee.

Each surgery I was instructed to stay on crutches and put no weight on the leg that was operated on for three weeks. When the second three-week period ended after the second surgery I was then instructed to not do anything that would put impact on my knees such as running or jumping for at least one year. I could walk, swim and ride a bicycle if I was careful but nothing else.

Two days later on the Saturday following my first surgery back in March as I was lying in bed at home recovering from the operation on my right knee which was the first of the two knee surgeries, my mom noticed something in the 2001 spring edition of BYU Magazine. I don't know how we got this magazine into our home; it wasn't addressed to us. I had never read BYU Magazine before.

On page 58 there was an article called, "Standards, Sportsmanship, and the Spirit" written by Willard Hirschi, who was a BYU track and field coach. The article was about when you forfeit your standards and integrity to win then you don't actually win.

I learned that in 1954 the BYU basketball team was having a losing season. Fourteen games into the season and BYU only won three games with eleven losses so far. At this juncture one player in particular did his part to shine his light along with his teammates to help change attitudes and improve work ethic which resulted in a complete turn around for the team that season. The team went on to win the remaining majority of their games and finished in second place in their conference.

The name of the particular player was Herschel "Bones" Pederson.

"Herschel 'Bones' Pederson?", I thought to myself in amazement.

My mom pointed out to me that this was the same Herschel Pederson who talked to me in the temple.

This is not a coincidence!

He told me to pray and ask Heavenly Father to help me to make my dreams come true. And when he told me that, there is no way he could have known I was already praying ever since I was little to make my basketball dream come true in addition to other dreams.

On top of that there is also no way he could have known my dream I was praying for was to play basketball at the highest level. I never said a word to him about that. And he is a basketball player himself! He never said a word to me about that. No wonder he was so tall.

And his nickname was "Bones" and the problem with my knees are with my bones.

This article also said: "Interestingly, 'Bones' was one of those, rare for his day, returned missionaries."

When I met him it was because I was going through the temple for my first time in preparation for my mission. And now I am a returned missionary just like him preparing to play basketball at the college level just like he did.

    Throughout my entire journey to make my dreams come true God has been there with me, and He is there with you, especially during the most difficult times. He has been there from the beginning to now, revealing Himself and helping me through the gifts and talents of others to "just hold on a little longer…"

CHAPTER 8

"I'll BE THERE"

From my journal, Friday July 5, 2002:

After work I called the basketball office at the University of Utah on the phone and left a message to find out the exact dates of the walk-on tryouts. Eric Jackson called me back and left a message on our home phone while I was gone shooting 500 jump shots.

When I played the message back, Coach Jackson introduced himself as the assistant coach, said he wanted to talk to me, find out what high school I played for and who my coach was.

Jackson was on the other line when I called back so I left a brief message. A few minutes later I called again because I was anxious to explain why I didn't make my high school teams due to my concern that when coaches find out I didn't play on my school teams it increases the possibility that they will look at me through different eyes than if they knew otherwise. I left a lengthy message recounting why I never made my high school team and that I will never quit.

"If I lose twenty games in a row, I'm back the twenty-first game," I said on the message. "If I go to the playoffs nineteen straight years, I'm back the twentieth year. If I'm forty years old, I come back the forty-first year!"

The machine ran out of time to record so I immediately called back again just to leave my phone number and this time Jackson happened to answer it.

He asked me what high school I played at and who my coach was?

"I never made my high school team," I hesitantly told him and briefly explained some reasons why but emphasized, "I will never be stopped. I'm like Stockton and Malone. I never quit."

Coach Jackson seemed impressed and said, "Coach (Majerus) may never even learn your name," and that, "there's going to be a lot of hard times," and "you may never play."

"That's awesome," I replied.

He said the tryouts would be during the first couple weeks of October on a Monday and Tuesday.

As the conversation was coming to a close Jackson said, there are probably going to be about 50 players trying out.

"50?", I asked, "Five. Zero?", making sure I heard him correctly.

"Yes, 50," he confirmed. And then explained the coaching staff is going to choose anywhere between two and five guys or they may not even choose anybody.

"I'll be there!", I promised with my whole heart because those are the kind of odds I like.

"If I don't make the team this year, I'm back again next year," I continued. "If I don't make it that year, I'm back again trying to make a semi-professional team. I'll be there!"

I returned by riding my bike to the courts two miles away and practiced 300 more jump shots until the sun set.

90 percent of success is showing up!
...Simplify for success.

90 percent of the follow-through or the finish is simply to show up to the starting line to begin with.

When you choose to be there by showing up, God will also be there. Do your best and God will do the rest. As well, God tells each of us: "I'll be there." And because God is there we each are given the power to be there. "I'll be there" is a team effort between you and God.

15 players, not 50, in total including myself showed up to the open walk-on tryouts for the University of Utah men's basketball team on Monday October 14, 2002.

Earlier in the year on Friday April 5, 2002 I tried out at the open walk-on tryouts for Utah Valley State College (UVSC) and at that tryout there were about 70 players who showed up. No one was picked to make that team.

The difference in size between the University of Utah (U of U) and UVSC is most likely the primary reason why less players, which were 15, showed up at the Utah tryout compared to the approximately 70 of those showing up at the UVSC tryout. The University of Utah is a four-year school and a bigger basketball school than UVSC which is a two-year school. At this time the U of U was regularly winning their conference championship annually and routinely ranked as one of the top 25 teams in all of college basketball.

Don't say something can't be done before you even start. Don't doubt in yourself before you even try. Don't think because the odds are against you or because the size of the obstacle seems too big to overcome that the dream at hand is too difficult to win. As long as you are trusting in God every good thing you desire will happen sooner or later.

90 percent of success is in your mind and in your heart. 90 percent of the effort, of doing your best, of never giving up is in your mind and in your heart. Just keep showing up and 90 percent of the race is already won.

Rewinding back to May 2001 when Dr. Kimball instructed me not to do any exercises or activities for twelve months that would cause impact on my knees, I now had to change plans accordingly because I couldn't play basketball for a year.

Originally the plan was to attend Snow College, a two-year school in Ephraim, Utah, because my chances would be higher to make the team since less players should show up in perceived theory to a tryout of one of the smallest schools in Utah. Then after making the team I could garner some attention during the games each season of some four-year schools and transfer to a university team. However, due to the fact my knees needed to heal by allowing the dead and newly reattached pieces of bone to resurrect and grow back to life, it didn't make sense to go to Snow College anymore. I wouldn't be able to play basketball there this year and by the time my knees healed I would be almost done with my education at Snow and it would be time for me to transfer anyway for my degree in journalism. So I went to the 2001 summer semester at Snow being that I was already enrolled for those classes and then in the fall I transferred to UVSC in Orem, Utah. Attending UVSC cost less than Snow since it was closer to home which saved me the cost of renting an apartment at Snow.

    I showed up to the pool, while at Snow in the summer, to swim one mile each weekday to get in as good of shape as I could and to strengthen my knees. Since my knees were weak, the speed of my swims were very slow but I just kept moving until crossing the finish line.

    At my six-month checkup in November 2001, Dr. Kimball said my knees were healing faster than expected so I could slowly start doing impact activities again like running and jumping but ideally I should wait until March 2002 before returning to normal impact activity.

"I'LL BE THERE"

    I showed up to the gym each weekday to either ride the stationary bicycle, or climb the stairmaster for 20 minutes at a time.

    I showed up when the first week of March rolled around alternating between weightlifting workouts on Mondays, Wednesdays, and Fridays and plyometric exercises on Tuesdays, Thursdays and Saturdays.

    I showed up on Monday March 18, 2002 to start playing basketball again since the first surgery last March. I played Mondays and Wednesdays in the basketball class taught by Coach Ray Stewart, the UVSC assistant coach.

    I showed up in January to cover a UVSC home basketball game for the school newspaper and interviewed Stewart after the game. And I asked him how does someone tryout for the UVSC team? Stewart asked me where I played high school basketball? I hesitated but slowly answered him that I never made my high school team and he looked surprised so I said, "but don't you worry about that." Stewart invited me to come play at his basketball class he teaches if I wanted to when my knees were ready and told me the tryout would be during the first week in April.

    I showed up to the UVSC open tryout Friday late afternoon April 5, 2002 where there were about 70 players competing to make a spot on the team. I was already transferring to the U of U and I was not in shape yet but went to gain experience for the upcoming tryouts at the U of U this fall. No one out of the 70 trying out made the team.

I showed up each day between May and October, running or biking in the mornings one and a half miles to the gym and back the same distance for a round trip of three miles. Weightlifting at the gym for 60 to 90 minutes at a time Mondays, Wednesdays, and Fridays. Performing plyometric workouts Tuesdays, Thursdays and Saturdays. Working at Kentucky Fried Chicken in the afternoons. Swimming half a mile every afternoon after work. Running or biking in the evening two miles to the outdoor courts at Barratt Elementary and back, for a round trip of four miles; to practice jump shooting between 300 and 1,000 shots as well as to practice ball handling through drills and exercises. Sundays I rested.

From my journal for the week of Monday July 8, 2002 to Friday July 12: I shot 1,000 jump shots on Monday, 1,000 on Tuesday, 500 on Wednesday, 1,000 on Thursday and 450 on Friday before severely spraining my right ankle playing in a one on one scrimmage that afternoon. That's a total of 3,950 shots for that week. The injury was to the same ankle I sprained back in January 1998. This current sprain prevented me from being able to do my plyometric and most of my cardiovascular conditioning exercises for four weeks. I did keep swimming though and lifting weights but I had to customize the weightlifting around the injury. To prevent any more severe ankle injuries, I started wearing ankle braces from that time forth.

I'll detail some of my weightlifting workouts later as now I will highlight my plyometric condition-

ing. Plyometrics are neuromuscular exercises which improve or quicken timing and athletic ability of muscles. My plyometric workout on Tuesday that week consisted of 3 sets of 1 minute each of:
1. Side to Side Box Jumps
2. Multiple Box Jumps
3. Box Jump 180's
4. Depth Jump Tucks
5. Arm Movement Box Jumps
6. Footpass

I use various box heights from a low of 24 inches up to a high of 42 inches or sometimes higher to leap over or jump on top. Depending on my weekly scheduled training regimens, I would do less or more sets than this current week.

My plyometrics for Thursday consisted of 4 sets of 1 minute each of:
1. Box Step Ups
2. Split Jumps
3. Medicine Ball Tips
4. Leg Drop Lunges
5. Knee Up – Tuck Jumps
6. 1-2-3 Drill

And that Saturday would have been, if not for my sprained ankle, 5 sets of 1 minute each of:
1. Line Drills
2. Hexagon Drill
3. Ankle Flicks

4. Side Hip Drill
5. Arm Movement Box Jumps
6. Footpass

When fall semester started at the end of August, I increased my workouts by adding on sprints. I ran 10 sprints each of 100 meters distance during lunch or between classes at the U of U. Or at home in the evening or early morning I would run 10 sprints of about 150 meters repeatedly up a steep hill. I also woke up at 5:30 am and depending on the day I would either run three miles on the surface streets or sprint one mile around the track at American Fork High School, followed by doing as many pushups as I could, eat breakfast, pray, and take the bus 35 miles to and from the U of U. I would usually be the only one out on the streets or the track at those hours.

After church on Sunday October 13, 2002 my dad wanted to give everyone priesthood blessings; Mama, Polly, Pat and myself. My dad gave me a blessing that I would be filled with energy, that I would feel this energy and that I wouldn't get discouraged no matter what happened at the tryouts.

When I went to bed at 6:00 pm I prayed, as I do every night, and again asked Heavenly Father to help me make this team.

I awoke at 4:00 am on Monday October 14, ate breakfast, prayed, my dad volunteered to drive me, we drove the 35 miles from American Fork and arrived at the Huntsman Center in Salt Lake City, Utah at 5:00

am. While waiting for the coaches to arrive I threw up my breakfast onto the grass because of the nervousness building up inside me.

I'm here.

I showed up.

I'm back again...

We did a lot of running drills. The three man weave, the five man weave, a three on two fast break drill, and a two on one drill. We ran and ran, over and over, again and again. I was loving every minute of it. This is exactly what I prepared and trained for. This is it!

Two defensive slide drills, some shooting drills, followed by the shuffle; which is an offensive system of movements to get your teammates open.

After 90 minutes of running and drills designed to see who was in shape, we scrimmaged in games of five on five. There were actually 11 players, not 50 as earlier predicted, who showed up on this first day with one having to leave early.

We played two games and I kept focusing on being the first one up the floor on offense, the first one back down the floor on defense and on who I could set a screen for each trip up. This continuous movement resulted in layup after layup on fast breaks and cuts to the basket created from screens that I set for my teammates. I was on the skins and both games I estimated our team outscored the shirts about 20 points to 10. I contributed between 8 or 10 of our team's points each game I estimated.

The shot of the day was when I positioned myself on the low post near the basket, turned to shoot and got bumped out of bounds. As I was falling out and away I shot from completely behind the glass backboard. The ball flew straight up over the top and dropped back down the opposite side of the board right through the hoop. Everybody stood there looking in amazement among the 15,000 red empty silent chairs of the Huntsman Center and I playfully yelled out, "And the foul!"

Another memorable play is when I brought the ball up on a fast break, faked the defense out with a fake pass which opened the lane for me to take it all the way to the net for the coast-to-coast layup and score.

Especially during the second game everyone was running really slow due to exhaustion of all the prior running drills and I was starting to get tired too but I kept thinking to myself again and again, "just keep moving" which enabled me to continue to be the first one up and down the floor.

Observing and coaching us at these open University of Utah tryouts were Eric Jackson and Scott Garson, who both were assistant coaches. Jackson said he and Garson weren't necessarily looking for the best overall player but for specific things that would make the team better in the practices this season and help the team win.

I am now twenty-three years old, six-feet four-inches tall, as I've grown another inch since my senior year of high school five years ago; now weighing about 190 pounds and being a junior in college. Even though I'm in my second calendar year of college I am technically a junior, rather than a sophomore, based on the number of course credits I've completed thus far.

Tuesday October 15.
I showed up.
I'm here.
Day two.
Again at 6:00 am we started off running the three man weave, the five man weave, the three on two fast break, the two on one fast break.

There were 15 players there on this second day and I was actually the tallest.

We did more defensive drills, one on one defense and rebounding, and three on three defense versus offense.

Lastly we played our five on five scrimmages and in between games we worked on the shuffle again that we learned from yesterday.

Everyone was even more tired than yesterday and I kept thinking to myself "just keep moving" until the finish.

Coach Jackson told us, "This is the best walk-on tryout I have ever seen."

He said he would post the names of who made the team on the basketball office door by 10:30 am.

Then he said anyone who doesn't make the team but loves basketball, loves being around basketball and still wants to be part of the team can be an equipment manager if they want.

As we left the Huntsman Center all of us who showed up genuinely congratulated one another on each doing our best. We each gained respect for one another and wanted to let each other know that showing up and giving everything we had says a lot about each individual here today.

Nervously as 10:30 am approached I made my way back from one of my classes to the basketball office.

Here we go again.

Seeing a paper taped to the glass, I slowly approached the office door while reminding myself that no matter what happens, "I did my absolute best."

There were five names listed on the white sheet and my name was not to be seen.

I stood there in silence and gathered my thoughts. I said a prayer in my heart saying to God, "You know I did my best, I did everything I could possibly do. Thank you for helping me."

I felt that Heavenly Father was thankful for me and for my effort.

I went in to talk to the coaches and Scott Garson was really happy to see me as he called me by name, "Hey Tim!"

I told him I wanted to be an equipment manager and he was genuinely excited as he motioned for me to come into one of the offices and sit down to talk with him.

"First of all," Garson said. "We just want to say that we just think you have had the best attitude the entire time. We can really see that you have a desire and a passion to play basketball and that you'll do whatever it takes."

"Really?", I said.

"We've never seen anyone love basketball as much as you do," Coach Garson said.

"Thank you," I said.

He said they have been very impressed with me and that I had the best effort out of anybody and I worked exceptionally hard.

He really made it a point to stress that my effort was very impressive and that I just out worked everybody.

They highly considered me to make the team and that "we almost made you a walk-on for your rebounding ability alone," he said.

"Oh, you think I rebounded well?", I asked with surprise.

"Absolutely," Garson confirmed.

I was a little surprised they recognized my rebounding skills since most coaches in the high schools I attended didn't seem to notice those non-flashy things.

I asked him if I played so well how come I wasn't picked as a walk-on? He said that I'm not quite big enough to be a big man. I let him know that I wasn't trying to be a big man. And he answered that my lateral quickness on defense needs to be better to be a guard in college.

I made a mental note that I was going to heavily work on improving my lateral quickness these next twelve months in time for the tryouts next October.

And to help bring understanding to the situation, my right ankle was still swollen since it had not yet fully healed from spraining it in July and my knees will never be normal as Dr. Kimball told me after my surgeries, so I might appear awkward in some of my movements.

I also want to clarify what is a "walk-on". There are two definitions. One definition is: any college athlete on a sports team who is playing without a scholarship. The other definition, which is the one I use, is: any player who makes a college team from an open tryout and is not recruited.

There are college players who don't have scholarships but are still recruited to be on the team without having to go through an open tryout. I don't consider them walk-ons. I consider them non-scholarship recruits. A walk-on is someone who is not recruited and instead makes a college team by way of a tryout.

"We almost even put your name on the list as a side note: 'Tim McGaffin, come see the coaches', because we really wanted you to be a manager," Garson continued. "But we didn't because we didn't want to make it look like we were excluding anyone else and because we were almost 100 percent sure that you would be coming in to see us about becoming a manager. We can tell you'll do whatever it takes."

A winner will do whatever it takes, as Scott Garson correctly recognized, only as long as it is good or right. A winner doesn't cheat. I want to make that perfectly clear.

After Garson explained what my duties as a manager would be, I asked him if he thought I ran the floor well? I told him I had a goal to be the first one up the floor on offense and the first one back on defense and I asked him if I accomplished that goal?
"Absolutely," he exclaimed. "We could see that you weren't necessarily the fastest guy out there, but that you were working harder than anybody else to get up and down the floor. You simply just out worked everyone else."
Practice starts at 12 noon.
I got dressed and down to the hardwood floor of the Huntsman Center ready to go. Right away the players started reaching out to make me feel part of the team. As Garson also told me earlier, "we're a family". Britton Johnsen for instance spoke to me as if we were already friends and said I looked familiar to him and he thought maybe we already knew each other from somewhere.
I didn't realize it until later but me and Britton

did meet back on the first day of school on August 21, when I went to check out the auxiliary gyms so I could know where I could practice between classes. In one of the courts Britton, Trace Caton, Richard Chaney, Tim Drisdom, Bryant Markson and Michael Doleac and one or two others were playing pick-up games. I stopped in to scout out my future competition of who I would be playing with and against in the upcoming practices this season once I make the team from the tryouts. I fully planned, worked, prepared and kept showing up every day and therefore I believed I would make the team. 90 percent of success is in your mind and in your heart. Keep praying!

As one of the managers it was my responsibility to get the players water, keep the floor dry, help record and film practices, help in anyway possible, and always have a towel and ball on hand.

Garson earlier told me there would also be times where I would be able to play in the practices. I was determined to make the most of every opportunity to get into the practices to get better and prove myself.

One of the practice sessions I got into today was where I fed the ball inside to the centers, the tallest players on the team, by way of an entry pass from the outside wing down to the low post, as they worked on offensive and defensive positioning. On one play I hit Chris Jackson with a no-look, cross-court floating lob pass, perfectly timed to catch the defender off guard for that split-second and just out of his reach so Chris was able to quickly catch and score.

"Nice pass man, nice man," Jackson sincerely said.

"Thanks," I calmly replied, while inside I was saying in my mind, "Yes! That pass and score was perfect! Just as I planned!"

Out of the 15 players who tried out to make the team as a walk-on, I was the only one who showed up to become an equipment manager.

Just show up.

I was amazed the minute Rick Majerus, the head coach, promptly arrived onto the floor at noon at how professional the practice was. Just like me, the players set screen after screen after screen, helped each other, communicated, encouraged and supported one another.

"Now that's basketball! This is great!", I thought to myself.

Majerus and each player, coach and manager was serious about each doing their best, about fulfilling their full potential, about winning.

I was loving every moment.

Finally after all these years, this is the closest I have come so far at being a part of a real team that took winning, and becoming better and improving and being a champion as seriously as I do.

The thing I loved about Rick Majerus is how he absolutely every single practice all season long always without fail spoke about the importance of: "never giving up" and "never quitting" in your life. Majerus was always talking about never giving up! Now that's basketball!

He spoke about his dream to play in the NBA and just make enough money to be able to support his family. He said he didn't need millions, all he needed was thirty thousand dollars a year to play basketball with the best players in the world and he would be in Heaven. I had a great feeling come over me when I heard him talk about this dream of his during one of the practices because that's my dream as well and I could really relate.

I learned that, like me, he too never made his high school team every year he tried out either and he too never gave up. Majerus went on to play college basketball one year which was his freshman year. He tried out and made the team at Marquette University as a walk-on. He said his nickname was "Rick the Pick" because he set picks or screens as well as could possibly be done.

After the practice on Saturday October 19 while talking with a lot of the players in the locker room one of them asked me, "Why are you so happy?" And I replied, "Because I can never be stopped. I get back up every time."

Practices during the fall usually went from 12 noon to 3:00 pm. And from 3:00 to 6:00 pm in the spring. The only days I didn't attend were Sundays.

I loved the feeling of simply being in the locker room with everybody. Just the camaraderie and team atmosphere of being with others who respected and understood each other.

"I'LL BE THERE"

On Tuesday October 22, a week after becoming a manager, I asked Trace Caton after practice where they lift weights and if he thought I could workout with the team? "Yeah," Trace said. "Talk to Britton because he's going over there today and he'll give you a ride."

On the drive over Britton told me about his tendinitis operation and I told him about my knees.

Arriving at the weight room where the U of U college athletes of various sports workout Nick Jacobson and Britton introduced me to Jason, the strength and conditioning coach of the weight room, and I asked Jason if I could lift weights with the basketball team and he nodded his head yes. I told Jason I would start lifting this Thursday with the team.

I'm not officially a player on the team but simply because I keep showing up, success keeps following through. Don't let imaginary doubts stop you.

Just show up.

Britton was impressed because this was the first time he knew of an equipment manager weightlifting with the team. Nick and Cameron Koford were joking that it's all down hill after twenty-three (years of age). "Nothing can stop me," I declared with a smile. And Britton said, "You got a dream!"

That's right. Go after your dreams.

Later in the season, I encouraged a couple of the five walk-ons to use the weight room and they decided not to because they were afraid they might be intruding. I told them they're on the team so they have a right to use the weight room if they choose. This is why I say 90 percent of success is in your mind and in your heart. You have the power to choose, no one can stop you from choosing. Make the choice and commitment to be unstoppable.

When Thursday came, me and Richard Chaney planned to meet to lift weights together at about 4:30 pm. When I arrived, Richard actually just finished lifting since there was no practice today so he started earlier and he waited for me. He stayed and let me know, "we're on your time." Richard took me all around, showed me what exercises to do and how to do them correctly. He was my personal trainer. I was very impressed at how the men on this team reached out. That's what teamwork is all about.

Throughout the season and off season I did all of the same weightlifting workouts as the team plus I added on additional exercises. If you want to be the best, learn from the best and do what the best do. Keep showing up.

Earlier in the week during the first of two practices on Monday, whenever the team had to run sprints repeatedly up and down the floor, I decided to jump in and run with them every time as well. I didn't ask permission from anyone, I just did it. And I kept doing so every practice while the walk-on players sat and watched from the side.

After practice Wednesday the team asked me why I kept running sprints with them? I said, "Because I'm doing whatever I can to be the best player I can be, and I'm not going to let you guys get in better shape than me."

Then I said, in addition to running sprints, "When they (the coaches) say, 'let's get another walk-on in here', I'm just going to jump in. They can't kick me out. Or maybe they can, I don't know?"

"Yeah," Trace Caton agreed with me. "No, they won't. Do it," he encouraged me sincerely.

That Saturday on October 26 after the second of two practices that day we had a team dinner at Mr. Mike Snyder's home. Britton gave me a ride.

"You know what I like about you Coach Majerus?", I asked him as I broke the silence of the room and him sitting on the couch and me standing in the doorway of the hallway.

"What's that?", Majerus asked me.

"I love how in those TV interviews you're always praising Stockton and Malone and pointing out how they can never be stopped because they never, never, never quit. You got to keep doing that. It's very important that you point out to people how Stockton and Malone never quit."

Then the other coaches there in that side room, Eric Jackson, Scott Garson, Kerry Rupp and Rick Majerus, upon catching the same excitement I was feeling whenever I think and talk about the greatest power in the universe, all started talking about the importance of never giving up and giving specific examples. "Never quitting" is contagious, it's an unstoppable power.

Once January rolled around I started consistently telling various players I was going to scrimmage with them in their pick-up games in the off season. I didn't ask permission if I could play with them, I clearly communicated I was going to play.

"I'll be there," is what I kept guaranteeing them.

After the pregame meal before Utah played BYU that Monday night on February 24, 2003, me and Trevor Jameson, who was the trainer of the team, got to talking as we walked back to the Huntsman Center from the hotel. I asked Trevor if he knew if walk-on players in the past have been able to practice in the off season scrimmages?

Trevor said that other people have tried to play during the summer with the players but they always end up sitting on the sidelines and never get to practice.

I thought to myself that the difference between me and those other players however is that I'm never going to give up all summer long. Even if I can only get into one full scrimmage, it will be worth it because miracles will happen. When you do your best, God will do the rest. When you exercise faith, God then works the miracle. What might seem like a small victory at the time nonetheless is a victory and could snowball into something huge.

To be clear, I was confident that in practicing with the players I would help make them better at basketball. I took this really seriously. This wasn't about me, it's about the team and helping each other get better. If I honestly felt I wasn't able to help make each other better yet, in practicing with the players, I would keep training and working and improving myself until I got to that point then.

And to be clear again, sometimes doubts enter your mind and you think you are not ready yet when you actually are. Even if you are not 100 percent sure of how things are going to go, don't let that hold you back from showing up. So much of barriers, walls, limits, or obstacles are illusions and you just got to break through the illusion.

"I'll be there!"

Tuesday April 8, 2003, I showed up to the East 109 auxiliary gym in the HPER facility. The season had ended a couple weeks ago with the loss to Kentucky in the second round of the NCAA basketball tournament.

The teams were six-foot ten-inch tall Tim Frost and six-foot four-inch Nick on one team versus six-foot four-inch me and six-foot ten-inch Britton on the other. We were playing two on two, first team to score 7 points wins, each two or three-point shot would be counted as only 1 point, and each time a team makes a shot they keep getting the ball back until the other team scores (you make it, you keep it).

Britton penetrated the lane, Nick left me to go help Frost cover Britton, at this moment I was left open and Britton fed me with a bounce pass. I scored on a right-handed layup. But it wasn't an ordinary layup, it was a Karl Malone layup; when the Mailman puts his left hand behind his head for a special delivery hammer dunk. I did the same thing, placing my left hand behind my head, except I laid the ball in off the glass instead of dunking it.

In reaction to my special delivery layup, Nick and Britton both stood there looking at me and then looking at each other with astonished looks upon their faces and both their hands behind their heads.

"It looks like you're trying to work a little magic there huh Tim," Nick said.

That exclamation mark I put on my layup was a little something extra to tell them: I'm here!

The next play I caught the pass from Britton on the left-side wing. I launched and made the three-point shot for point number 2 for our team. Remember even though it was a three-pointer, it only counts as 1 point in this scrimmage.

"Tim has some serious range," Britton told Nick since we both practiced together last week so Britton knew I could shoot.

Point number 3 came when I missed a difficult layup moving away from the basket on the left side but I got the rebound and put it back in the hoop.

Strongly dribbling from the left side of the court to the right lower block of the lane against Tim Frost resulted in me making a driving layup for point number 4.

Next I received another pass from Britton on the right-side lower post three feet away from the basket and I very quickly shot a high arcing rainbow over the outstretched arms of Frost so he couldn't block it for point 5.

"Tim, I'm just going to keep feeding you the ball. This is your debut," Britton announced.

I made a three-pointer on the right-side wing this time for point 6.

Then I made yet another three-pointer again on the right-side wing for the game-winner and point number 7.

Me and Britton won 7-4 with me scoring all 7 points.

Victory!

I went 3-for-3 on three-point shot attempts and 7-for-11 overall from the field. My four missed shots included a missed driving floating right-handed shot in the lane over Nick, a difficult reverse layup going from right to left, and the missed layup I put back in that I mentioned earlier. The fourth miss was a quick jump hook shot on the right side over Frost that I tried to bank in off the glass.

The complete sequence of shots went: Malone layup, made three-pointer, missed floater, missed reverse layup, the feed inside from Britton, missing the layup that I rebounded and put back in, the driving layup made over Frost, the missed bank hook shot over Frost, the made rainbow three-footer, and the two consecutive made three-pointers on the right-side wing to win the game.

Bryant, Tim Drisdom and Richard also showed up to play after my debut game.

We finished scrimmaging at about 4 pm.

I thanked everyone for the games and the practice and they all thanked me and said I played well.

"Nice job Tim. Really," Nick said. "You did really good. Seriously, thanks Tim."

"Yeah, good job Tim," Britton said after Nick.

"Thanks guys, I really appreciate it," I said hiding my excitement that I had done it. This was another dream come true! I played with some of the best players in the world and I played well.

During the season I got into the practices for a few minutes at a time doing drills but this was the first time I got to play in live games.

Everyone left to go weightlifting and Britton asked me if I would stay to practice shooting with him as he prepared to hopefully enter the NBA this June in the draft. We each took turns, rotating around the three-point line, shooting multiple sets of three-pointers until making ten each set. Britton made ten as I rebounded for him and then switching and Britton rebounded for me as I made ten.

Jason, the trainer of the weight room, asked me why I was late for weightlifting with the team and told me to do one-hundred up-downs (combination pushups). After completing fifty-two Jason told me to stop because Britton explained to him why I was late.

"When Britton wants you to rebound for him, tell him he can rebound for himself," Jason ordered.

After I completed the workout with the rest of team, Nick and Amy Jacobson offered me a ride to the bus stop. Before we entered the car I asked Nick if I looked like someone who never played in high school before?

"You never played in high school?", Nick asked me upon hearing this new revelation. He thought I played on my high school teams so I explained briefly about my history of getting cut from the teams.

Keep showing up.

Tuesday June 10, 2003. The teams were three on three, me and Nick and Tim Frost against Geoff Payne, Josh Olsen and Stefan Zimmerman. Bryant also was there but he couldn't play because he had an ankle injury that was still healing. Nick and Frost just kept feeding me the ball in a great display of teamwork and the score was quickly 6-0 with me scoring all 6 baskets counted as 1 point each. Nick was quick to remind the man guarding me that I was kicking his caboose. I then walked over to Bryant on the side sitting on the floor and gave him a high-five as we all laughed because here I was dominating and I never played on any of my school teams so this was another testament that the person who never quits truly is unstoppable. Me taking a moment to highlight this moment by giving Bryant five put the exclamation mark on this testimony of mine in action so everybody knew what was going on and where the power came from. What exactly is going on? Champions never quit. That's what's going on.

I was unable to make it a shutout though as they came back to make the score 6-3 before I then hit the game-winning shot, a three-pointer on the left wing, for the win 7-3 with myself again scoring all 7 points.

The next day we were playing four on four with the teams originally being me, Tim Frost, Geoff and Josh against Nick, Stefan, Bryant and Chris from the football team. My team had won every single game so far except for only 1 loss with about 15 wins. Frost called me a man-child since I kept boxing out and positioning myself to keep grabbing so many rebounds in very congested areas and over people taller and bigger than myself. "He's a man-child!", he proclaimed after I pulled down yet another rebound.

Because I was also scoring so much, a particular player on the opposing team switched with the man originally guarding me defensively. With this defensive switch the hope of our opponents was now that I would be slowed down. But I kept scoring on the new man guarding me too. The new man coached the guy who was guarding me prior on how to slow me down; but the man prior reminded the new man that I scored on him (the new man) too.

"I like this guy," I said playfully as I referred to the man prior because he was exactly right. So the solution was to try and even things out by putting me on the losing team and Chris on the winning team. With this switch the teams were now me, Nick, Stefan and Bryant against Tim Frost, Geoff, Josh and Chris. We decided to play a best of five game series so the team to win three games first, wins the series.

My new team lost the first and second games

and won the third game to make the series 1 win and 2 losses for us going into the fourth game.

In the fourth game we were down but we fought back to tie the score at 6-6. There was a scramble for the ball and Chris picked it up and rolled out of bounds. Me, Nick and Bryant all yelled, "OUT OF BOUNDS!" But Frost said Chris was fouled and pushed out. The discussion continued for at least five minutes as to whose ball it was. Finally an agreement was reached to shoot for it. They missed the shot so it was our ball.

I took the ball out from the top of the key and passed it to Nick on the right-side wing. The defense was intense. Everybody on both teams was giving absolutely everything they had left in the tank on this one play to win this game. Chris left me to go double-team Nick who was dribbling in place and drawing the defense out. I motioned for Nick to pass it to me for the shot as I was left open. Nick bounce passed it to me, I caught it above the three-point line and thought to myself, "I'm going to win this right here." I took one strong right dribble up to the free throw line and as Frost approached, I pulled up and perfectly knocked down the jumper for the win!

A full out celebration erupted! Bryant was doing a little dance on the left wing. We were yelling and screaming. I high-fived Nick and told him we ran that play to perfection! Bryant was still dancing and now singing as I high-fived him and Stefan.

We then went on to easily win the fifth game

and the series 3 games to 2. The team I was on lost 3 games and won about 18 games on the day.

Keep showing up.
Wednesday June 18, 2003. I was assigned to guard a star player who was voted the best high school basketball player in his entire state by the newspapers from the state he was from in the USA. He played the point guard or shooting guard positions which are positions the quickest players usually fulfill. We were playing four on four, full court at a school called Rowland Hall.

The leader of the other team, that my opponent I was guarding was on, coached everybody to let my man play one on one against me. He told everyone to let my man isolate against me. All the players then moved completely to the left side of the floor to give the man I was guarding a lot of room on the right side to maneuver and drive his way to the hoop for what should be a relatively easy score against even the best defenders.

I got extremely low in my defensive stance as I awaited my man to make his move to attempt to drive against me. I was secretly very excited inside because I knew I was going to totally shutdown my man with my defense because I had been working on my defensive lateral quickness since the tryouts last October. My goal was to become the best defensive player on the entire team.

My man drove to his left over to the baseline

and I cut his path off completely. He was going no where. He backed up to where he started from to reset and then tried driving baseline again and again I completely cut off his path. He then tried to get past me by driving to the middle of the floor. I focused on only two things. First, staying extremely low. Second, staying in front of his stomach. I just looked at his stomach, never looking at his head or his limbs because if you concentrate on the extensions of the body you can get faked out as the head or an arm or leg can move quickly one direction while the body moves the other direction. If you just look straight at the core of their body which is their stomach and ignore all other movements you will not be fooled as to where they are actually moving. As he drove to the middle of the floor he attempted a myriad of moves but made no progress against me so he passed the ball back out.

    The leader of the other team said something to the effect of, "okay, that didn't work." So he then coached his team to let my man isolate against me again and to again drive against me for what should be a relatively easy score. The ball was passed back to my man and he again tried to drive past me going left, right, left and each way he went I stayed low and in front of his stomach and again I shut down the entire play.

    Multiple players commented on how impressed they were with my defense. I could see the wheels turning in some of their heads as I know some of them were trying to figure out how it was possible that I had never made my school teams or this team yet from the walk-on tryouts last October as I was definitely outplaying yet again another star player.

The very first play offensively for our team I out ran the entire defense up the floor and Justin Hawkins hit me in stride with a perfect pass and I laid the ball in off the glass for the score.

The next trip up the floor I again out ran the entire defense and I received another nice pass from Justin that resulted in another easy shot and score.

After those two consecutive fast breaks where I out ran the defense Nick Jacobson asked my man that was guarding me if he was "hurt or something?" My defender said "no" and Nick told him, "Tim is faster than you."

The secret is that I was simply working harder. Not just working harder during these games but each and every day. Each day showing up to the weight room to lift, showing up to the gym to train, showing up to the court to practice, showing up to the track, street and hills to run, showing up to every opportunity to get better.

It's the effort that matters. What matters is that you keep trying, that you keep getting back up.

Or as Yoda in Star Wars says: "Do or do not. There is no try."

When Yoda said that in The Empire Strikes Back, I kept trying to figure out what he meant by "there is no try." I realized he meant to do what you have control over. You have control over your effort.

"I'LL BE THERE"

Do your best! Don't try your best. Do your best! As long as you keep doing your best, all obstacles will be overcome sooner or later with the help of God.

Another opponent dribbled the ball up the court and I could tell by the movement of his eyes as he approached me that he was planning to fake a shot and then pass the ball to the star player I was guarding. So I faked his fake. By this, I mean I acted like I really thought he was going to shoot it. I acted like I fell for his fake shot and as he began to pass the ball I scooped it right out of midair and I took off sprinting the opposite direction. I was gone, dribbling coast to coast for the layup.

Next I grabbed a rebound, my man that was guarding me tried to steal the ball away from me, I did a crossover dribble and blew right past him. I was gone going the opposite direction leading yet another fast break. I hit Justin with a perfect pass he caught in stride to knock down an easy short jumper.

Next I cut down the lane in the middle of the court and Stefan Zimmerman hit me at the perfect time with a sweet pass just when I got open in the passing lane. I then leaped into the air, released a floating shot based on a well timed and calculated trajectory where my body is flying through the air and simultaneously I float the ball over the outstretched arms of the defenders and softly through the net.

Some players had surprised looks on their faces even though they have seen me make these difficult shots multiple times by now. So I playfully declared,

"That was all skill!"

These difficult shots are ones I practice regularly because there are times where you need to make adjustments in midair. Those who lack the skill will mistakenly call it luck because it appears too difficult to be planned.

The very next play down Justin passed the ball to me immediately on the right wing. Speedily I dribbled straight at the defender near the hoop. With only inches to spare I abruptly changed from full speed to slow motion to avoid colliding with him and then I patiently muscled in the layup high off the glass making it impossible for the opponent to stop.

"That was all skill again. Slow motion skill," I declared again as some of us laughed.

Next, yet another cut to the rim on the right block where I called Zimmerman's name. Stefan threw me another perfect pass that I jumped up, caught in midair and shot into the basket all in the same motion before landing. Perfect teamwork!

Tim Frost wasn't able to scrimmage today because he was healing from a surgery on his nose so he watched from the sidelines.

When we finished playing and walked off the court, Tim Frost broke through the momentary quiet of everyone cooling down as he declared to the team while speaking directly to Nick, the team captain, something to the effect of, "Well Tim (referring to me) tore it up."

"I'LL BE THERE"

Keep showing up.

My goal was to work harder than anyone else on the team so that I would have a chance of becoming the best basketball player on the team. I wasn't even on the team yet but regardless, my goal was secretly to become the best basketball player on the team. With that type of attitude, you may not always get exactly what you want at a certain time but still good things are always going to happen. And, I know without a doubt I did work harder than anyone. No one worked harder than me. There may have been someone who worked equally as hard as me but there is no way anyone worked any harder than I did. My daily goal was to work myself to exhaustion.

For instance, after working out with the team on July 2, as I walked over to get my bag, the assistant strength and conditioning coach of the weight room came over to me and wanted to shake my hand. His name is Matt Balis. In a few more months he would be promoted to the head coach of the weight room. Matt said he wanted to congratulate me on how hard I'm working and on my attitude. We had just finished our team workout moments earlier with a rock race. This exercise consisted of the basketball team being split into two relay teams where we did a series of sprints while carrying huge rocks weighing 70, 80, 90, or more pounds. I was the fastest person on both teams during this race. Matt told me, "I know you are going to go far in life because you have what it takes." And he went on to explain that I was working harder than anybody on the team. He said I was out performing athletes that were supposed to be bigger, faster and stronger than me simply because I was working harder than them. Matt was very sincere and genuine and it was very inspiring. I knew that he could see me and it really meant a lot to me that he really cared. He told me he believes I can make the team.

For my training I was doing the exact same workouts that the team was doing, the same weightlifting and abdominal or core strength workouts. The weight sessions were filled with lots of squats, cleans, presses, and pull-ups. But in addition to what the team did, I was also running three miles almost everyday. Sometimes I would sprint one mile instead of run three. If I wasn't exhausted by the end of the day I would go do some more running or sprinting up some steep hills. I was running more than anyone on the team. I was doing my plyometric workouts three times a week that no one else on the team was doing. I was playing basketball between one and three hours a day, five or six days a week. I rested on Sundays. And I was riding the bus 35 miles to and from during the season. During the summer I drove my car instead of taking the bus. This extra commute time took away from time I could have used to swim half a mile a day as I did in past summers. I was also working part-time at the bread mill of Russ Callister during the summer.

When I tested my vertical jump in June, I measured 28 and a half inches on my standing vertical jump and 32 inches on my approach vertical jump. Even with my surgically repaired knees, my vertical was higher than a handful of players on the team. And in the area of flexibility, I was the most flexible one on the team. My flexibility measurements were the best of everyone.

Two specific exercises I was doing three times a week that no one else was doing either was the sumo squat and the stability ball wall squat. This was a routine I came up with myself to do after the weight-lifting workouts. I did these exercises specifically to help me reach my goal of becoming the best defensive player on the team. These squats strengthened my legs so I could stay extremely low in my defensive stance for extremely long periods of time with ease. Because of my less than normal knees I needed to strengthen my legs to the highest levels humanly possible to try and make up for the lack of proper knee function.

The sumo squat is done by standing in a wide stance with your feet usually much further apart than shoulder width. I would then hold either a 55 or 65 pound weight in my hands. Then you squat down keeping your head and chin and chest up to ensure your back maintains straight posture so you don't hunch over and hurt yourself. You don't want to do more weight than you can easily handle. Play it safe. As you squat down you keep your hands holding the weight dangling between your legs. Squat until your legs reach a 90 degree angle when bent at the knees so your thighs are parallel to the floor and your shins are vertical to the wall.

Stability ball wall squats are very similar. A wall squat is where you sit against a wall with your back flat against the wall and your legs at a 90 degree angle like you're sitting in an invisible chair. The longer you sit against the wall the more of a workout your quadriceps or thigh muscles receive. When you put an inflatable exercise ball or stability ball between your back and the wall, you then can squat up and down against the wall as you roll up and down against the ball. Make sure you keep your back vertical and parallel to the wall.

Depending on the day I would do between 1 to 3 sets of 30 repetitions of sumo squats and between 1 to 3 sets of 60 repetitions of stability ball wall squats. I would usually start off with a 55 pound weight and then change up to a 65 pound weight on the second set onward.

Looking at these numbers on paper doesn't capture how difficult this amount of weight and reps really are. It might not seem like it would be that difficult to some people until you actually do these exercises yourself. Some days I was dreading doing these two exercises at the end of my workout. The only way I continued to make it through each day was by praying and asking God to help me. This would always help me feel Heaven close by and motivate me to continue to improve and keep going.

When you get to 15 or 20 reps on just your first set your thigh muscles are already burning like crazy. You can't stand it. I just kept pumping away with extreme focus until I got to the end of the set by completing the 30 or 60 reps. As well, I would many times let out a big holler upon completion of each set.

Just doing 1 set of either of these two squat exercises would be enough to exhaust me. But I would keep doing them until I overloaded my thigh muscles to failure. What I mean by failure is that you work your muscles to complete exhaustion. This is no exaggeration when I say that I could not actually walk for a few minutes by the end of the last set. I would hobble over to the floor mats and lay down for a number of minutes until my legs regained enough strength to stand up properly and walk again. My legs would be shaking for quite a while afterward from the completion of these two exercises alone.

My plan was to condition my legs to withstand the highest levels of burning and fatigue like it was nothing when compared to doing those squats. Therefore I would be able to easily stay in my basketball defensive stance for extremely long periods of time, get lower than anyone else defensively and be able to guard anyone.

Keep showing up.
Wednesday July 9, 2003. Today we were scrimmaging at the Zions Bank Basketball Center, which was the current name of the practice facility of the Utah Jazz of the NBA. I was told that only players officially on the team of the University of Utah were invited to come to the facility and practice with the Utah

Jazz players...

...I still showed up.

I practiced shooting on a neighboring empty court as the players of the Utah Jazz and the official players of the Utah Utes practiced.

I decided to keep a positive attitude and not let myself get discouraged that I wasn't able to play in these games even though I had already proved myself countless times in these off season scrimmages.

Gordon Chiesa, assistant coach of the Utah Jazz, was in attendance observing along with Gary Briggs who is the trainer of the Jazz.

The Jazz players there were Raul Lopez, the point guard from Spain who was coming back after major knee surgery, Sasha Pavlovic, Mo Williams, and Curtis Borchardt, the seven-foot tall center who was coming back from foot surgery. And there was a bald guy from Europe that I'm not exactly sure who he was. The Ute players there were six-foot eleven-inch tall Chris Jackson, Justin Hawkins, and Bryant Markson. Geoff Payne and Josh Olsen both were also there and had to leave early.

Jazz trainer Gary Briggs approached me midway through one of the first scrimmages and told me to go in.

"I need you to go in for Curt," Briggs said.

"For Curtis Borchardt?"

"Yeah, he took a fall and today is his first day

back playing so I want you to trade for him," he said.

I took off in a mad sprint to switch my white t-shirt and put on my number 11 Utah Utes old practice jersey my sister Pollyanna acquired and gave me as a gift. I wanted my family to be there and triumph with me so that jersey was symbolic of them being there with me. To further help the visual of how I appeared when I played all summer long, I wore red practice shorts and my haircut was the ultimate basketball haircut called the flattop.

Gary called over to Curtis and told him I was trading with him.

I sprinted onto the main court and got extremely low in my defensive stance: Here I am.

I'm back again.

As soon as we got the ball back on a rebound, I got open and a player hesitated to pass me the ball. Raul told him to pass it to me. Raul understood what basketball is all about and was great to play with because of his true love of the game.

Playing four on four half court, the teams were me, Raul, Sasha and the bald guy from Europe versus Justin, Bryant, Chris and Mo.

My first shot came when I caught a pass on the left-side wing inside the three-point line, just above the elbow of the free throw line with my back to the basket. I reversed pivoted to face the basket and shot the ball with confidence. It missed off the back of the rim.

"Good shot," Raul told me even though it missed.

My second shot came when I expertly positioned myself to grab an offensive rebound in heavy traffic. In one swift motioned, I boxed out, timed the miss, I went airborne, grabbed the rebound, shot the ball as I was still in midair and descended back to the hardwood. The moment I released the shot, before I even landed, my teammates got excited and cheered my effort. Somehow the ball barely rolled out though. But regardless of the miss, multiple players remarked how impressed they were because of the high-degree of difficulty to even grab that rebound in such tight quarters in the first place and against players physically bigger than myself. As well, I was impressed how these guys got excited about the same things I get excited about; the things that matter.

My third shot came when Sasha was on the right baseline towards the corner of the court and inside the three-point line, trying to drive along the baseline. I was on the left side wing. The lane below the free throw line was open space. I cut to my right towards the free throw line, slowed my steps for a split moment acting like I might be attempting to set a screen which put the defense to sleep, and swiftly cut past my defender and into the lane. Sasha hit me with a pinpoint timed pass as I entered the open lane space. In a split second before the defense closed in on me, I shot in stride a seven or eight-foot runner, banking the ball off the glass and in through the hoop for the score!

"Hey. Good job," Raul said as he pointed to me. I pointed back, nodded my head and smiled.

My fourth shot came when Raul drove from the left side wing down to the left side baseline. Simultaneously, parallel to him, I cut down from the left side elbow of the free throw line down to the baseline near the basket. Raul connected with me on a perfectly timed pass and when I turned to shoot it off the backboard, I got bumped and Justin blocked the shot.

Later, one of the opposing guards was on the right baseline with the ball in his hands and Chris was on the opposite left baseline. I was up from Chris, away from the baseline and towards the free throw line, at about the midpoint between the free throw line and baseline, guarding my man. I read the body language of the opposing guard with the ball and could tell he was planning on faking to pass one way but then give Chris a no-look bounce pass behind the basket along the baseline in the hopes of feeding Chris to score a wide open layup or dunk. So I faked his fake. I acted like I wasn't paying attention so I could bait the opposing guard to implement his plan. He took the bait. Here came the bounce. Patiently I timed my movement to wait until the ball was completely out of his hands. And to the surprise of many I seemingly appeared out of nowhere right in front of Chris to steal the pass away with a huge smile on my face and to the tune of gasps of frustration from some opponents. That was a big play late in that scrimmage that helped us win that game as it got us the ball back to score on our next possession.

"Yeah, you're real good," Chris Jackson said to me with the highest level of genuine respect when we finished playing and as we were walking over together to get a drink of water.

"Thanks Chris," I said simply with humble gratitude.

Raul Lopez also told me, in his Spanish accent, that he thought I played really well and he sincerely wanted me to know that. And everyone else let me know that I played well too.

I couldn't stop smiling.

I had done it!

This was a dream come true.

I played with NBA players for the first time ever!

I was jumping up and down on the inside but on the outside all you could see was a never ending smile.

I highlighted a small amount of plays but every play was a highlight to me. My favorite part was that I still showed up despite being told I was not invited to play, then destroyed the obstacles and performed undeniably well. I proved once again that so much of the walls built up to stop us are illusions and we only need to break through and break down the grand illusion by continuing to show up and be there.

When I got home that evening I told my dad and he said, "It was all meant to be."

Poppy explained the fact that I never played on the team in junior high or high school but now after all these years I'm playing with NBA players proves that

"I'LL BE THERE"

God is with those who never give up.

I knelt down and prayed, thanking Heavenly Father for helping me and that I knew I could not have done it without Him.

Before the day was over I went running another one and one-third miles.

This was not the last time playing NBA basketball, this was just the beginning and the best is yet to come. I remember specifically later in July when Michael Doleac, who was currently playing for the Atlanta Hawks in the NBA, played with us and he got really excited about my hustle. There was a rebound barely out of the reach of my hands and just within reach of my fingertips. I kept tipping the ball repeatedly to keep it away from the hands of an opponent. Each time I jumped as high as I could to tip the ball and keep it alive Michael cheered, "yeah!", "yeah!", "yeah!" He was so sincere as he told me multiple times throughout the scrimmages how impressed he was with my effort, hustle and teamwork. This is what basketball is all about.

I kept a solid daily record of the scrimmages we played throughout the off season including the wins and losses. Some days however, I did lose count on how many wins exactly the team I was on would achieve since we consistently won more games than we lost. This is why on some days in my journal I say we won "about" 18 games for example. Because the number could actually have been 19, 20, or 21 since I sometimes lost count once we got on a roll. I wrote down the numbers after all the games were over for the day rather than during the games themselves. So my recording of the amount of wins is not exact but it is very close. According to my daily record, the team I was on won at least 70 percent of all the games. I say "at least" because it is not exact and there is a high probability the percentage of wins is higher than 70 percent.

Winning at least over 70 percent of all the games whenever I am on the team is not a coincidence. It is not an accident that the team I am on consistently wins a significantly higher percentage of the time.

In basketball and in life:

Keep moving.
Keep helping.
Keep a positive attitude.
Keep having fun.
Keep winning.

...Keep praying.

A few times during the season a couple players asked me how it was possible the coaches didn't pick me to make the team from the tryouts. They said they thought from how I performed in the drills during the practices that I looked like I should be on the team.

I replied that I didn't understand and was confused but grateful to be given this opportunity to be an equipment manager and still be part of the team.

Then during the off season after actually playing with the team and proving myself in actual scrimmages instead of limited drills, many players expressed disbelief that I was not picked to make the team from the tryouts. Many thought I deserved to be on the team based on the winning results of my performances this summer.

Keep showing up.

Tuesday August 12, 2003. During my weightlifting workout today Alex Jensen, who I practiced with during some summer scrimmages, was there and asked me for an update.

I told Alex that there are already 16 players on the team. The coaches told me that they can't keep more than 16 players even though last season there were a total of 17 consisting of 12 recruits and 5 kept from the tryouts. But this year because of NCAA (National Collegiate Athletic Association) rules, the men's team cannot have more than 16 players because of something to do with how many players there are on the women's team. For the first time in the fourteen years that Rick Majerus has been coaching at Utah, the team brought in an extra 4 recruits in addition to the other 12 recruited players. The 5 players kept from the tryouts last year were not asked to return to the team this year. Unless something changes the coaches aren't even going to keep one player from the tryouts this year.

I explained how frustrating the situation was but that I'm also not going to give up. I've done everything I possibly can within my control and now I need to trust in God that everything else will take care of itself.

Alex told me firmly not to give up. He told me to stay with it and that something will happen.

He said in case he doesn't see me before he leaves on Friday to play basketball in Turkey this season, that he believes in me and hopes everything works out for me in making the team.

"Thanks Alex, I really appreciate it," I said.

Keep showing up.

Wednesday August 20, 2003. Today was the first day of classes. At 1:00 pm I went to my appointment to talk to Coach Eric Jackson in his office about the tryouts.

I sat down in the chair and stated to Eric, "I'm ready. Let's go. Let's do it. I'm ready to do this."

I told him I understand they already have 16 players. He explained they can keep one more if the women's team has more.

Then Jackson told me that they may not even have tryouts this year but if they do it will be held on October 20 and 21 at 6:00 am.

I was a little shocked by this when he said they may not even have tryouts at all.

"You better have the tryouts," I told Jackson defiantly. "Even if you don't keep a single player, you need to have the tryouts if nothing else so I can be there to compete and do my best because this is what I've been working so hard for this entire year again. I don't care if nobody shows up and I'm the only one. I'm going to show up and I'm going to be there."

Then I told him I don't want to be a manager. I didn't want to be a manager last year but that's not to say I wasn't grateful for the opportunity because I am grateful to be part of the team. I just don't want you to think my goal is to be a manager. My goal is to make this team, play on this team and help us win.

Then Jackson told me, "I want you to understand that it's not always the best player that makes the team."

He explained that what they're looking for are players that are going to help the team out during practice by fulfilling a certain function that they are looking for.

"We loved having you with us last year," he continued, "and we want you back again with us this year in whatever capacity that may be. Whether that be a different capacity like the one you're looking for or something else."

Jackson also knew I scrimmaged with the team during the summer but it's against NCAA rules however for coaches to watch team scrimmages in the off season so he, nor any other coach, ever saw me.

After that conversation with Eric, being that the

chances were high there wasn't going to be an open tryout held this year, I consistently went to the basketball office a couple times each week to stick my head in to ask Eric Jackson or Scott Garson or both, if we were having the tryouts yet. Each time the answer would come back similarly as, "not yet." And I would follow-up each negative prognosis with a reply similarly saying, "well, I'm ready", or "well, I'm going to be there."

About eight weeks straight of receiving negative notices with one week left, I received word this time when I stuck my head in the office that the tryouts were now going to happen.

Keep showing up.

Monday October 20, 2003. I woke up at 4:00 am, ate breakfast, prayed, left at 4:47 when I looked at the clock, arrived to the Huntsman Center at 5:24 am. Eric Jackson got there about 10 minutes later. I went to the bathroom, then to a room to be alone to pray as I got my ankle braces and shoes on. 11 players in total showed up. Two of them were Mike and Trevor, who tried out with me last year. Another player trying out was someone already on the football team.

I remember Mike because I thought he should have been one of the players who should have made it along with myself. I remember he was the smallest player in physical size but he worked extremely hard. I saw him after the tryouts last year and told him I thought he should have made it. I asked him if he was going to try out again and he said, "probably not" and

I encouraged him that he should try out again.

We started off running with the three man weave, and then the five man weave.

Last year I was the tallest player at six-foot four-inches and this time there were 4 others my height. The players were bigger and better competition than last year.

Next we did a drill where a man at the top of the key had the ball and a man on the wing would cut to the low block near the basket and come back up to receive the ball and then drive and lay it in. Next drill he would pass it back to the man at the top of the key. Next drill we added in a head or shot fake before we drove it to the baseline and bounce passed it to the corner three-point line and that person would shoot a three-pointer. The timing and precision of my cuts were excellent and my first two shot fakes Eric said I was going too fast so on my third fake I slowed it down and Eric said that time was perfect.

Next we did a three on three defensive drill. When I got into my defensive stance I was lower and wider than any other and I could tell from the looks on the faces of Eric Jackson and Scott Garson they were impressed. The goal of the drill was to get three consecutive defensive stops in teams of three and then trade once three straight stops were achieved. The team I was on kept getting stops but we couldn't quite get that third stop. After a while Scott said, "Okay, let's get another group."

"No, we're going to do it," I called out.

"You're going to do it?", Scott asked me.

"Yeah."

Garson kept us in then and we got the three stops.

A local television news station was there, channel 2 KUTV, doing live segments of the tryouts for their morning show. I was a little bit upset about it though for multiple reasons. One of those reasons was because they interrupted some of our drills.

We continued to do variations of defensive drills in teams of three on three and five on five until 7:30 am when we divided into teams of five of shirts versus skins to scrimmage for the remaining 30 minutes. We played full court and the coaches called the fouls.

I was on the skins team and we won both games. We won the first game 9-8 and the second game 5-4 with each basket counting as 1 point.

In the first game my team was playing too fast and out of control so I told everybody to "slow it down." We kept playing too fast so the second time I said, "we need to run an offense, we're playing too fast." I don't know if Eric heard me but he called timeout and called just our team over. He told us that he was happy to see us pushing the ball but we were playing out of control. Mike was on the other team and they were beating my team 5-0 at this point. After we slowed it down our teamwork was much better and we came back to win 9-8.

In the second game we were up 3-1. Mike's team came back to tie the score at 4-4. Eric announced "next bucket wins." I got the ball on the left wing, faked a three-pointer, my man jumped and I took one power dribble to my right followed by two gigantic steps into the lane. I went airborne at the dotted line of the circle below the free throw line and soared in for an explosive right hand layup for the game-winner.

Upon landing I let out a cry of victory!

"Yeah!", I cried out.

That shot got more reaction from Eric Jackson and Scott Garson than any other play that I noticed.

I turned around and stood there triumphant.

Eric said, "You should have finished that play off like Michael Jordan and stuck your tongue out."

Eric told us that this year was better than last year which was the best year ever for tryouts until this year became the best ever. He told us to sleep in as a reward and come back at 6:30 am tomorrow. Before we left he handed us a play to memorize for tomorrow.

Keep showing up.

Tuesday October 21, 2003. I was the first player to arrive again this morning. There were 9 players who showed up today, two less than yesterday.

We started practicing the play we were handed yesterday. Eric had me play the forward position and then the center and then forward again in that play set. I knew the play better than anyone that I could see.

Next we lined up along the sideline and dropped down low into our defensive stances and slid along the entire perimeter of the court. Eric made me the lead-off man. I was lower and wider than anyone else. After a while some players started to really struggle but for me I was having a lot of fun and could have continued sliding around the perimeter for the rest of the tryouts without any problem. That's how easy this exercise was for me because of the specialized training I went through since last October for this very purpose.

Next we did the three man weave. Then a two on one defensive drill. Then we practiced setting screens. Me and Mike were both setting excellent screens. Then we worked in teams of three in bringing the ball up the floor in the point guard position, then pass the ball, set a screen away from the ball, cut after setting the screen, receive a pass, drive to the hoop as a man follows behind and pass it back to the follower. We kept doing that drill repeatedly until we could do it perfectly three times in a row.

Then we played three on three with the first team to score 5 buckets wins. Me, Trevor and Mike were on the same team. We scored 4 buckets in a row. We weren't able to score on our fifth possession. So we then went on defense and rotated through the lines until we were back on offense and we scored our fifth basket for the win when I grabbed an offensive rebound and put the ball in.

Next we played three on three again with different teams but this time we had to rotate through the lines each time instead of playing each made bucket consecutively. Only the point guard could dribble on the initial drive. After he picked it up nobody could bounce the ball and we had to pass and score from cutting and setting screens. The team I was on lost this time because our teamwork was lacking. One player on our team was trying to score from home run plays. A home run play would be one where you do something absolutely amazing but what wins is consistently doing the little things and not the big flashy things. And when you consistently do the little things or in other words, "keep moving", the big amazing plays will follow through and happen anyway.

Finally we practiced playing in a zone defense with five men on defense and four on offense. As soon as the five on defense got five defensive stops, four men would then go onto offense.

The first go around I played center on defense and we got five stops.

Then on offense I was positioned on the wing and we passed the ball around way too slow around the perimeter. I was trying to get us to really whip the ball around quickly and this is when Eric called timeout and asked us what the key is to scoring against a zone defense?

"Quick ball movements," I answered.

At this point I went back on defense and we got five defensive stops again. Still no one had ever scored on offense yet in this zone drill.

I went back on offense. I boxed out two guys at one time in an attempt to get an offensive rebound but the ball bounced the other direction. The next play I boxed out two guys at once yet again and this time I pulled down the offensive rebound and Eric and Scott were really getting into it as they were cheering me and that rebound like crazy. Right after that I positioned myself inside to create enough space to receive a pass and shoot a nice jump hook that missed off the back of the iron. Next I got another offensive rebound which I put in with a nice turnaround jumper resulting in the first score of this zone drill.

The very next play I sealed off my man and Mike threw me a perfectly timed floating pass that I jumped towards while at the same time keeping my man sealed. And while holding that seal I turned inside to face the hoop as I simultaneously caught the ball and laid it in for the second score of this zone drill.

"Nice pass Mike. Nice pass," I declared as I pointed back at Mike and he pointed to me.

That play got a lot of reaction from Scott and Eric too.

"Nice seal!", Scott yelled, and Eric decided to bring the team in. Those were the only two times anyone scored in that zone drill.

Gathered around in a team circle, Coach Jackson asked us, "What do you do when you pass the ball to the wing?"

"Screen away," I answered.

"What happens when the help defense comes over?", Eric asked.

"Somebody else is open," I answered.

Then he told each of us, "If you show the same

dedication that you showed here in whatever you go on and do in life, you're going to be very successful."

"Tim here, was a manager for us last year and this has been a yearlong process for him," he said.

Then we brought it in tight, bringing our hands together and cheered: "Team Together."

Eric told me to come to his office tomorrow to find out if I made the team.

I congratulated Mike on his effort again and told him he played just as good as last year.

That night I called Nick Jacobson to see if we have practice tomorrow because I'll be there in one capacity or another. Amy, who was a star player on the women's Utah team for four years, answered the phone. She said she saw me on television Monday morning when channel 2 was doing their report live. She said the exact moment that the camera showed us playing I got a steal and led the fast break, passing it down to my teammate for the score on a layup. She said I looked great and hopes I make the team.

Then Amy asked, "Did you hear about Britton?"

"Did he make the team?"

"He made it onto the Orlando Magic!", she said excitedly.

On Wednesday I hurried to Eric's office after class and when I got there I said, "Hey chief." And he told me to come in and close the door behind me.

I sat down and he asked me, "How are you feeling?"

"Nervous," I said and then smiled.

"There's no reason to feel nervous," he told me.

Then he told me straight out that they decided to go with Mike and there's only room for one and "that's it."

Jackson said, "Mike came in here a little while ago and I explained to him that it's not a glamorous position just like you know it's not a glamorous position. And we told him that if he didn't accept the position then we were going to put Tim on the team..."

"...You were our number two man."

I felt a lot of different emotions all at the same time as I walked out of the office. When I got outside in the crisp autumn air I began walking the half of a mile to the weight room to do my workout. As I walked alone, I also felt alone so I started praying. I told Heavenly Father how discouraged and frustrated I was feeling and how I didn't understand. As I kept directing my thoughts to Heaven, I felt God close by my side. I wasn't alone. I felt that He was very proud of me and thankful for me.

"Any other year you would have made it except for these recruits this year," Chris Jackson said to me the next day during the practice on Thursday. Multiple players told me the same thing before and after this practice that I came back as an equipment manager.

I thought for sure I was going to make the team this year. When it didn't happen I was definitely confused and things definitely didn't make sense at the time but through it all I know God was definitely with me. I know with all my heart that God hears and answers all of our prayers. He doesn't hear some and answer some. He hears every single one and answers every single one. There will be many times however when there doesn't seem to be an answer readily available and where it seems God is not hearing or answering our prayers. In these times keep showing up. Keep praying. As you continue to exercise faith you will continue to gain understanding. God knows all things and has all power. We each can only see and understand a part of the whole plan that will continue to reveal itself as we continue to exercise faith or as we continue to exercise "never give up".

On that day when I was nine years old that Heavenly Father answered my prayers and told me I should play basketball, I made the commitment to myself and to God that I would never give up no matter what happens.

To you, who is reading this very sentence right now, remember who you are and never give up no matter what happens because the best is yet to come for you. God will continually be with you as you continue to not give up.

CHAPTER 9

KEEP HAVING FUN

If you're not having fun, you're doing something wrong.

In whatever you do in life, it should be fun if you have the right mental attitude.

In the summer of 1990 when I was still ten years old I attended the basketball camp of Utah Jazz player, Thurl "Big T" Bailey at the Orem Recreation Center. I won the "Best Ball Handler" award at that camp. I was the only kid there who could dribble the basketball between and through their legs while walking up and down the court. My ball handling was something I was having fun working on, through the practicing of various drills since last summer.

I'll never forget the first day of camp when Thurl Bailey taught us that when he receives a pass and makes a shot he always points back to the man who gave him the pass to thank him for the assist and teamwork.

He taught us that you need to have fun by supporting and helping each other and cheering each other on. I could see he was really serious about that.

Ever since then whenever I make a shot after receiving a pass from my teammate I always point back to them and thank them for the pass. As well, when I make a great pass and they score from it, I point to them and get excited about the teamwork.

Thank you to all of my teammates I have ever had. You know who you are. I wanted to get all of your names and recognize all of you in this book because every true teammate I have ever had is a champion. You have helped me so much to keep coming back. You know who you are. Thank you forever.

I was born at home with the help of a midwife on August 23, 1979 in Provo, Utah.

August 23, 1987 to August 23, 1988,
Eight years old,
Second grade at Scera Park Elementary in Orem, Utah:
I started praying, asking God what I should do in my life. I actually started praying a few months prior to August of 1987 when I was seven years old. I kept praying...

1988-1989,
Nine years old,
Third grade at Scera Park:
My prayers were answered in September of

1988. The answer was to play basketball and become the best basketball player ever.

Immediately I began practicing every day after school.

During recess at school I tried to start playing basketball with the other kids but I almost never got picked to play on a team. On the rare occasions that I did get picked, I was usually picked last.

Many kids did make fun of me a lot too when I was little. I didn't care about being popular or conforming. I cared about being myself and doing the things that I like to do. I liked to draw a lot and do artistic and creative things. I didn't play any sports except for soccer during recess in first grade. I obviously didn't like being made fun of and not being included to play basketball with others. I promised myself that I would do my best to not make fun of others and to treat others how I would like to be treated. As well, I promised myself that I would not exclude others from playing basketball because everyone should be allowed to play and get better and have fun. Basketball is about everyone being included, not excluded. On the rare occasions that I did make fun of someone however, I would remember my promise and go sincerely apologize to them which would make everything great between each of us again.

I also started getting my flattop haircut towards the end of this year. The flattop is the ultimate basketball haircut. A lot of basketball players had this haircut where your hair stands up vertically high on top of your head and cut flat and shaped square on the top. The hair on the sides and back of the head is cut short. I wanted to get my hair cut like this because I really liked the artistry, the toughness, the strength of the cut. I felt inspired to get the flattop. When I tried to figure out why I felt inspired to get my hair cut like this I realized it is because the flattop is an outward expression of "never quitting". The lines are strong, tough, consistent, constant, persistent, persevering, unbreakable, unstoppable, and invincible. Sometimes people ask me if I'm in the military because the cut is short like military-style cuts. I say that I'm not in any earthly military but I am in God's Army just like you. Each of us lived with God before we were born and we were each saved to be born on earth at this time in the final stages of the war that began in Heaven. This war is the war between good and evil, liberty and slavery. No matter how hard things may seem or how dark the hour may appear, the final victory will be for liberty! Let's do it.

1989-1990,
Ten years old,
Fourth grade at Scera Park,
Four-feet eleven-inches tall,
Weighing about 75 pounds:

    I played in my first organized basketball league called Junior Jazz, named after the Utah Jazz. It was the local city league. Anybody that wanted to pay the registration fee could play. My dad coached our team.

We practiced setting lots of screens to get each other open and passing the ball to the open man. We practiced teamwork. My dad coached us to learn what basketball is about. I remember my first game of the season I had 16 points. I revealed my hook shot that my dad helped teach me how to do correctly. I really enjoyed being part of a team and working to become better players and teammates. It was a lot of fun!

In the summer I went to the basketball camp of Thurl "Big T" Bailey which was my first ever basketball camp and was so much fun!

1990-1991,
Eleven years old,
Fifth grade at Scera Park,
Five-feet tall,
Weighing about 85 pounds:

Last year I noticed the sons of the football and basketball coaches of Orem High School were on a superleague team instead of playing in Junior Jazz.

I found out there was going to be an open tryout for the fifth grade superleague team.

The tryouts were held in early November at Orem High School. On the first night which was Monday, the coach of the team, Steve Downey, taught us how to do left-handed layups. Most of us were right-handed. With all the shooting I had been practicing the last two years I never thought about shooting with my left hand. On the second night while we were warming up I worked on practicing my left hand layups. I felt extremely awkward shooting with my weak hand but I was determined to keep working on it, to get better. One of the sons of one of the high school coaches started making fun and laughing at me.

He asked me, "Why are you practicing left hand layups for?"

"So that I can get better," I answered.

"You're never going to need to shoot those in games. You're wasting your time," he said and continued to say how they are too hard and how funny and goofy I look when I shoot with my left hand.

And I replied that they're always going to be hard and feel awkward until you keep practicing to get better.

The tryouts went all week with a cut after Tuesday, a cut after Thursday and when we finished playing on Friday, Coach Downey said he would call us this weekend to tell us if we made the team or not. There were quite a few kids at the start of the tryouts. I would estimate the number to be about 35 or more.

Saturday passed and there was no phone call. Then Sunday came and went into the evening.

The phone rang.

Coach Downey sounded really happy and then he told me I made the team! Practice starts tomorrow at the high school and he gave me the time to be there.

As soon as I hung up the phone I told my family and started running and jumping around the house. It was the happiest day of my life so far. All the practice had paid off. My plan to play in the NBA was right on track. All I have to do is keep making the teams each year and work my way up.

During the season Steve Downey told me the main reason he chose to put me on the team is because I am the best shooter. And he said that I was one of only a few players who actually keeps his elbow straight and aligned with the basket when he shoots.

I really loved playing on the team. I loved my teammates. Every practice was so professional and so much fun because I was getting better and learning a lot. I was so happy being on this team and practicing and playing in the games. And we won a lot of games. We were one of the best teams in the superleague.

1991-1992,
Twelve years old,
Sixth grade at Scera Park,
Five-feet one-inches tall,
Weighing about 95 pounds:

We didn't have a tryout for the sixth grade superleague team. We brought back all the same players as last year and added on two additional players to the team. Everything so far is going according as planned.

In the spring of sixth grade is the first time I noticed something wrong with my knees. Normally I played basketball every recess, but this particular week I was taking a break for a couple days and playing Frisbee football. At the end of one of the games I reached out to catch the Frisbee disc and something happened in my knees. I suddenly couldn't bend my knees, it felt like it had locked up. I stood there and couldn't move. I somehow laid myself down onto the grass without bending my knees and a couple of my friends were concerned. After lying on the lawn for some time, I suddenly was able to move and bend my knees again. It was strange.

1992-1993,
Thirteen years old,
Seventh grade at Lakeridge Junior High School,
Five-feet three-inches tall,
Weighing about 105 pounds:
    An idea came to my mind.
    I began exclusively using my left hand every time I picked up, carried, held, or handled anything such as books, folders, papers, meals, groceries, the trash, opening doors and drawers, and everything else to improve the control and strength of my left hand to equal that of my right hand. Every minute I wasn't playing basketball, I was playing basketball if that makes sense. The more I increased the control and strength of my left hand to match that of my right hand, the more ambidextrous I became so I could handle, dribble and shoot the basketball on the same level as I could with my right hand. Even to this day whenever I pick up, carry, hold or handle anything I use my left hand solely. The only time I use my right hand is if I have too many things for one hand and need to use both.
    The tryouts were held in early November at

Orem High School. I hardly ever got the ball no matter how many times I got open. Not many kids would ever pass the ball. Most of the kids would force up bad shots whenever they got hold of the ball. I kept waiting for the coaches to step in and instruct us on passing and working together as a team but the coaches never coached in this regard. I also thought the coaches would notice that I was not concerned in getting shots for myself but instead I was concerned for getting good high-percentage shots for the team, whether that be me or someone else, so we could win. I kept passing, even though I wasn't getting passed to myself. I also noticed the coaches weren't really paying attention. They were often talking to each other on the sidelines while we scrimmaged instead of watching and observing and teaching us.

At the end of the second night of play, the names of the players who made the first cuts were read aloud. There were about 60 kids at this tryout.

One by one the names of who made the cut were read...

...Tim McGaffin.

I made the cut.

I made it to the last day of a week of tryouts which was a Saturday. As we scrimmaged, the coaches were nowhere to be seen. They came out when we finished playing in the morning and then read the names of who made the final cut.

My name was not read.

I believe the player that was chosen instead of

me made the team for a couple reasons. First, he was bigger and stronger than me. We were both the same height but he was bulky and I was skinny. The position the coaches wanted me and him to fulfill was the forward spot which is usually where the bigger or taller players fill. My basketball skills such as rebounding, ball handling, passing, shooting, decision making, were superior to my opponent but he was physically bigger than me. I thought the coaches would recognize the importance of positioning, timing and skills over physical size but they chose otherwise. The second contributing reason I believe my opponent was chosen instead of me was because his dad was one of the coaches as well.

    I did my best to keep a positive and thankful attitude and keep things in the proper perspective but it was hard. I was really hurting inside for a long time that I didn't make the team especially since I had worked so hard.

    For the season I played Junior Jazz again in the city league and I played in the church basketball league. My dad coached our Junior Jazz team again like he did when I was in fourth grade. It was a lot of fun especially since Scott Hansen, my best friend, was on our team and Scott made a lot of three-pointers. I played the point guard position which is my favorite because I love passing and distributing the ball and helping to get everyone involved and having fun. One practice in particular that was a lot of fun is when my dad required ten pushups from anyone who missed a layup.

On the last day of school which let out early, as soon as the bell rang, I walked the little over one mile journey to the Orem Rec Center to practice basketball for the rest of the day. From the very first moment, I was starting my summer off right, determined to practice every available minute and second of sunlight to get better and leave the coaches no chance not to pick me again to make the team.

My knees felt pretty good for the most part throughout the year until the summer arrived. I was attending the Mountain View High School basketball camp in June. On the last day of the camp we were playing some really fun full court games when out of nowhere my knees felt excruciating pain. I hobbled over to the bleachers and sat down. But when I tried to stand back up, I could not. I was stuck. The coach who was officiating our game asked what was wrong. After explaining how bad my knees were hurting and that I couldn't stand back up, he thought I was making the whole thing up because just minutes ago I was one of the best players on the court. He thought for such a sudden change to occur was impossible and that I must be lying instead.

I started crying as I yelled at him, "I can't even stand back up!"

After about 10 to 15 minutes of not being able to stand, I finally was able to raise myself back up very gingerly. I walked slowly out of the gym when my dad arrived.

My dad was really concerned and thought it might be related to growing pains that sometimes happen during growth spurts.

1993-1994,
Fourteen years old,
Eighth grade at Canyon View Junior High School,
Five-feet six-inches tall,
Weighing about 120 pounds:

For hours on end I played and practiced basketball most weeknights and Saturday afternoons at the Orem Rec Center during this time. On one particular Saturday I had one of the greatest shooting performances in basketball history when I made at least 15 three-point shots in a row. It might have been more than 15 but I lost count. I was about fourteen years old playing five on five full-court pick-up games with the other nine players being in their twenties and thirties. We played probably between six to eight games with the first team to score 21 points wins the game. I made between two to four, three-point shots each game. My team went undefeated for the afternoon. It is very possible I could have made 18, 20, or more three-pointers but I lost count. At the end of the afternoon many of my teammates and opponents told me they had never seen someone make that many three-point shots without missing.

That performance went back to when I first started practicing when I was nine years old and made a goal visualizing in my mind having games where I would never miss a shot. Never say something good can never be done. All good things are possible and will happen sooner or later with the help of God.

Days later word had spread of this legendary performance of mine as multiple other players, who were not there on that previous Saturday, continually came up to me to tell me they had heard about how many three-pointers in a row I made without missing. They were genuinely happy and excited for me and for us because we are teammates.

Being seen on television doesn't make a performance legendary. Doing your best and having fun together with your family and friends makes what you do legendary. Also doing your best and having fun when you're by yourself training, practicing or exercising your God-given talents is also legendary.

I really loved playing basketball on countless nights and Saturdays at the Orem Rec Center. I played a lot with my dad too. Me and my dad made a lot of true friends and teammates. Everyone was included, nobody was excluded and we had so much fun.

As November approached I kept asking a son of one of the coaches at the high school when the tryouts for the eighth grade team would be. Again I asked him during a class we had together on Friday if he knew when the tryouts were going to be held yet? He said he still didn't know. I said it either has to be this upcoming week or the week after and "are you sure you don't know yet?" He assured me he didn't know.

On Tuesday, during this same class I heard him

talking with a couple other kids in the class about playing in some basketball games together. After a few minutes I figured out they were talking about the tryouts that had already started yesterday on Monday. I frantically asked him what was going on. Why didn't he tell me on Friday the tryouts were starting this Monday? He said he didn't know on Friday the tryouts were going to start on Monday. This was the same person I found out from when the tryouts were going to be for the fifth grade team that I made three years ago. We didn't have class on Monday since our class rotated every other day. I would have gone straight to the coaches of the eighth grade team itself and asked them except frequently the coaches of the seventh and eighth grade teams were different, chosen at the last minute, and separate from the junior high schools. Many times these coaches are also parents of their sons that moved on from seventh to eighth grade, so the coaches changed frequently from year to year accordingly.

    This is why I asked the son of a longtime coach of one of the team sports at the high school when the eighth grade tryouts were scheduled to take place. His dad would have information to when the gyms were going to be scheduled for the tryouts and his son, who I asked, was going to be on the basketball team as well and would need to participate in the tryouts to make his placing on the team official. Ultimately it is my responsibility to find out when the tryouts are scheduled to be held but I want to bring understanding to the situation that it is difficult to find out especially when I was on the outside of certain circles of influence.

That Tuesday night, I showed up to the second night of tryouts being held at Orem High School and explained to the coaches why I had not been there yesterday. As we scrimmaged for only about one hour I noticed the coaches were no where in sight for most of that time. Not only were the coaches again not paying attention, but they were not even there. They finally emerged to read off the names of who made the first cut and my name was not read.

When I arrived home I could not hold back the hurt any longer as I burst out crying tears of frustration and discouragement. I felt a lot of hurt since I put in all of this work and practice again for another entire year and after all of that effort I didn't even make it to the first night of the tryouts.

For this season then I played church basketball again and I also joined and played for a team in the AAU (Amateur Athletic Union) in the Salt Lake City area.

1994-1995,
Fifteen years old,
Ninth grade at Canyon View Junior High School,
Five-feet eleven-inches tall,
Weighing about 135 pounds:

I won third place in the entire school in a one on one tournament. Games were played with two opponents playing one against the other, and the first person to score 21 points wins each game. The tournament lasted about three days.

I would have won first place if it wasn't for my knees though. I went undefeated to become one of the final four players remaining in the tournament. Then I barely lost to the first and second place winners by just one or two buckets in each of the games between those two.

On defense I could not get as low in my defensive stance as my brain was telling my knees to get. My opponent then had an advantage to get around me easier when he dribbled the ball and drove on me because I was not able to cover enough space and block their path to the basket in my more upright defensive position. I could still block their shots from various side and behind angles and get deflections on the ball as they drove but a lot of their shots were relatively near the basket resulting in high-percentage opportunities for them to score.

As well, because my knees hurt severely, I had a hard time offensively driving on my opponent. For that reason I had to rely heavily on my outside shooting to score the majority of my points by making three-pointers. If my knees would have been functioning properly I would have been able to dynamically move and drive on offense, as well as defensively cover more space to make my opponents take more shots further away from the hoop.

When the tryouts came around, there were about 50 players trying out and I had one of the best overall performances of anyone despite the severe pain of my knees. Whenever I play basketball I start warming up, stretching and preparing my body and focus of my mind before anyone else. It takes me a much longer time to prepare than others because it takes a long time for my legs to get warmed up to a level that I can play my best possible.

There were kids that used to make fun of me a lot but after they saw how well I played both days in this tryout, they gained a lot of respect for me and we actually went from being rivals to becoming friends instead. That's how well I played.

Shockingly to my surprise and to the surprise of many others at the tryout, I didn't even make the first cut when I viewed the list of names posted on the gym doors Wednesday morning. So when school let out on that Wednesday afternoon I waited by the office of the head coach and when he arrived, I went to ask him why I didn't even make the first cut.

I wanted to know the specific things that kept me from making the cut so I could work on those things and get better.

Upon asking him what factored into his decision that kept me from making the first cut, he didn't have any answers for me and wanted to get ready for the start of the third day of tryouts that would begin here shortly.

I reminded him I won third place in the Canyon View one on one tournament and asked him how does someone who proves himself to be at least one of the best players in the school, not even make the first cut?

I asked him, "Didn't you see that the team I was on during all of the scrimmages always won?" I never remember losing a single game. "Did you notice my teamwork?", I asked.

I asked him, "Didn't you see how when I was on defense that the man I guarded always had less points than me every game?"

I asked him if he saw how many steals I got on defense in the games and in the fast break three on two drills?

I thought maybe he knew I had knee problems or maybe he thought I looked awkward as I played so my whole point was that it doesn't matter how someone looks on the outward appearance. What matters are the results. My results of winning in every game I played speak for themselves.

He never really answered my questions and said he had to get ready for the third day of tryouts.

For this season then I played church basketball again and Junior Jazz city league basketball again.

Our church ball team went undefeated and was one of the best in history as we won the 1995 championship. On that team, we had Richard McClure, who I thought was the best big man player in the whole school and who also didn't come close to making the ninth grade team; and we had Josh Goodrich who moved to Utah from North Carolina after the school tryouts. Josh was given a chance to practice with the ninth grade team since he arrived to Utah after the tryouts and he didn't make the team either. Josh scored 30 or more points in every single church ball game that season. Josh was also the best big man player in the whole school alongside Richard even though neither of them made the team.

Me and Richard also played together on the same Junior Jazz team. We reserved to practice at the Canyon View gym one night and the ninth grade team had just ended their practice before we began ours. We challenged the ninth grade team to a full court scrimmage. Not everyone on their team accepted the challenge but enough did so we could play five on five. We easily won the scrimmage.

After the season ended I wanted to get in better shape so I decided to join the track team and run long distance. I absolutely hate running competitively because it is extremely difficult and I have the absolute greatest respect for long distance runners because of that difficulty.

I focused on the fun though instead of the difficulty.

I visualized myself getting in better shape and how that was going to make me a better basketball player and how much fun it was going to be to perform at higher levels than ever before.

My specialty race was the mile run or 1,600 meters. I was the second fastest runner on the team behind Ryan Ormond. At many track meets, my most common finish was fourth place. Ryan consistently finished in first place.

I was one of the fastest runners mainly because I

just wanted to get the race over with each time. The faster I ran the sooner the pain was over. I say that jokingly but my knees really were in a lot of pain.

I won ninth place in the 1,600 meters in the state of Utah at the Box Elder track meet which was the biggest track meet of the season. I was in about fourth place as I entered the final 100 meter straightaway but I got passed by four or five runners at the end to finish ninth in the state. Ryan finished first in the state.

Shortly thereafter I went to go see the doctor about my knees. When I ran, I felt like I was swinging my legs out and traversing over ground as if my knee joints were weakly connecting my legs together with pieces of string. I wasn't able to push off and explode with bursts of speed which is what is needed to finish the race strong in the last 100 meters so you don't get passed from behind.

Upon examining my legs, the doctor said he thought I just needed to strengthen my thigh muscles by doing simple exercises like leg extensions for example. He didn't take any X-rays. I listened to what he said but I didn't agree with him. I thought there was something seriously wrong with my legs.

Another idea came to my mind.

I stopped drinking soda pop.

One of my running coaches didn't drink soda pop during the running season because he said it slows you down. So I thought if he doesn't drink it during the season, then I'm not going to drink soda pop at all anymore.

Eliminating soda pop completely from my diet has given my conditioning an increased level of health and performance. Not having all of that unnatural sugar like high fructose corn syrup and other unnatural and harmful ingredients in your body makes a measurable difference in the health of anyone.

I don't smoke or drink alcohol or take other harmful substances so it wasn't hard to also eliminate soda pop as well.

1995-1996,
Sixteen years old,
Tenth grade at Orem High School,
Six-feet one-inch tall,
Weighing about 145 pounds:

I kept running by joining the cross country team in the fall.

One word describes running cross country:
Torture.

I hated every second of it. But again I loved that I was getting way out of my comfort zone by doing something I hated, so this perspective of climbing the mountain made it fun.

My goal was to become the best conditioned basketball player in the entire school. Running eight miles a day on average with the best runners in the school definitely got me in my best shape ever so far.

However, like I said, it was torture especially since it was hard on my knees. The pain was always there every day and it just starts to numb your mind as you continually endure the hurt before, during and after running or playing basketball. The most frustrating thing wasn't the actual pain but the lack of being able to functionally move my legs correctly. This lack of function causes you to perform significantly lower than your full ability.

When running in practices or the three-mile long races, what kept me going when I felt extremely tired was praying and asking God to help me finish the race. These prayers always helped me to simply focus on following through to just get to the next tree, the next street corner, the next garbage can, the next fence, the next parked car. Once I got to that tree, corner, can, fence, car or whatever the target was, I then focused on getting to the next and the next until I got to the finish.

The basketball tryouts were held in early November with about 50 players showing up.

I never got tired.

My goal of becoming the best conditioned basketball player was realized.

But the coaches barely even watched what was going on. I remember playing scrimmages in the middle gym and looking around and there was not one single coach to be seen.

After two nights of tryouts, when I arrived at school on Wednesday morning to see the list of names that made the first cut, my name was not included on the list. This was the third consecutive year that I didn't even make the first cuts.

I went on to play church basketball and Junior

Jazz again for the season.

We won the championship!

Our Junior Jazz team this year was one of the best in history as we won the championship in the Utah Valley area which consists of Provo and Orem, Utah. My teammates on this 1996 championship team included Josh Goodrich, Richard McClure, Kevin Hill, Devin Spann, Jeff Turner, Andy Long, Bryan Peterson and myself, Tim McGaffin. Our team was coached by Kevin's older brother.

My favorite game, other than the one that won us the championship, was our double overtime victory during the regular season.

At halftime Kevin's brother made an adjustment and assigned me to guard the top scorer of the opposing team who scored the majority of the points for his team in the first half. That top scorer then in the second half, who I now guarded defensively, never scored again.

With 6 seconds remaining in the game we found ourselves down by 3 points. The other team had just scored again to increase their lead from 1 to 3 points ahead of us.

I looked over at the clock and saw 6 seconds left to play. We did not call timeout as I called for the ball, —being that I was our point guard— to be inbound to me. I dribbled the basketball up the floor with calm urgency. With 6 seconds left to go, the clear thought on my mind was, "I'm going to make the shot and win this right now."

There was never a thought of missing the shot. I made the decision and knew before I even took the shot that I was going to make it. I kept thinking, "make the shot".

As I dribbled the ball coast to coast, weaving through traffic from one end of the floor to the other, I acted like I was looking for someone to pass to by continually glancing at my teammates. This kept the eye of the defense asleep and away from me. When I reached the top of the arc of the three point line slightly left of center, I froze the defense in place with one subtle shift of my head and shoulders and a glancing look at the path leading up to the basket. The opponent directly in front of me froze and I rose. I released the ball from my right hand and followed through and as the ball hung in the air, I knew I had made the shot before it even swished through the net.

The moment the ball swished through the hoop my next thought was, "now let's win this game." I already knew we were going to win the game in the upcoming overtime as I focused and visualized what we were going to do to finish and win the game.

The entire 6 seconds moved in slow motion to me. After I made the shot, which was my fifth or sixth made three-pointer of this game, I was still in that slow motion world of thought and visualization because I didn't even notice the sound of the cheers of my teammates or our friends and family in the stands.

When I turned around and a bunch of my teammates jumped around me and on my back and shook me out of my slow motion world did I suddenly hear and see the cheers. I looked down the floor to the opposite end where the rest of our team was and suddenly saw everybody jumping up and down and celebrating like crazy. I suddenly heard the voice of Poppy, my dad, and I looked over at him on the sideline enthusiastically cheering me, "All right Timmy! All right! Great shot Timmy! Great shot! Yeah!" And I saw Mama and Pat and Polly celebrating too.

We remained tied throughout the first overtime and then we took a big lead in the second overtime and won the game.

I loved playing on this team because we were all about teamwork and having fun and that is why we won so much. Our games are just as important as any NBA game because we play the right way. It doesn't matter that our games aren't televised for the whole world to see, what matters is having fun. I finished with 29 points in this double overtime win but what I love as much, if not more than the scoring, is the passing. I love playing my favorite position which is the point guard position because it allows me to distribute the ball and get everyone involved and having fun; throwing no-look lob passes down to Josh and Richard in the post and letting them do their thing as they dominated inside; driving and penetrating the lane and then dishing the ball to Josh or Richard for the easy two-pointer; moving the ball to Kevin or Devin or Jeff or Andy or Bryan for the score. Me and Josh also ran the pick-and-roll play to perfection, where the man who doesn't have the ball sets a screen or a fake screen for the man with the ball which opens up so many passing lanes and driving lanes and open spots for good high-percentage shots. Me and Josh played so well together that we could read each other's thoughts. We knew what each one was thinking and what move or decision we would each make beforehand. When you're able to play together at such a high level of teamwork is when basketball really gets fun.

I also never got tired in any games this season because of my conditioning from running cross country. Keep moving! Due to my preparation I was able to keep moving every minute without needing rest when the hard times came or when crunch time came.

That's how we won the 1996 championship for the Provo and Orem, Utah area. We kept moving. We kept playing together and helping each other. We kept having fun.

The tournament that would determine the champion was double elimination, meaning a team would be eliminated from the tournament when losing two games.

We had to beat the same team twice in a row to win the championship since they were still undefeated until they met us. We lost one game earlier in the tournament, so if we lost another we would have been eliminated.

Both times we beat this team for the championship we won by large double-digits; we won by 18 or 19 points both games.

Our team with Richard McClure and Josh Goodrich and myself, who are three of the best high school basketball players in the Provo and Orem area, neither of the three of us came close to making our high school teams. Yet this team that we easily beat twice to win the championship had two players who made the eleventh grade high school team in the fall of 1996.

Also during the season there was a shooting competition called "Milk Sure Shot" where I recorded the highest score of the Provo and Orem area. You had about one minute to shoot to the tune of theme music from five different marked spots on the floor as well as two layups. You got extra points from shooting from each of the designated spots at least twice in addition to every shot you made. One of the marked spots was from the three-point line and as time expired, I launched and made my third three-pointer right at the sound of the buzzer. The scorekeeper had an impressed look on his face as he tallied up all of my points and then revealed to me I just compiled the best score of the entire contest.

A number of weeks later the top eight shooters with the highest eight scores in the Utah Valley area were invited back to compete at Timpview High School. The winner would go on to compete in the finals of the entire state of Utah which would be held at halftime of a Utah Jazz game at the Delta Center. On this night I finished with the second highest score out of the eight shooters. I was one person away from advancing to compete in the finals at halftime of a Jazz game.

1996-1997,
Seventeen years old,
Eleventh grade at Timpanogos High School,
Six-feet two-inches tall,
Weighing about 165 pounds:

    With my right hand pressing the ball against the side of my right hip, I jumped into the air and spun while airborne in a full circle three hundred sixty degrees around. As I spun clockwise on the low post block on the right side, I simultaneously released the ball from my hip at about the peak of the jump and midpoint of the spin so that the ball flew sideways and connected square in the hands of my teammate situated on the opposite left side block on the low post. As the ball flew across, I continued spinning until I completed the full circle fly. My surprised teammate, because of how I passed the ball to him so unexpectedly, was wide open and made the easy three-footer layup. No one on the court had ever seen a pass like that before. Most of the players paused for a few moments, replaying in their minds what they had just witnessed to make sure their eyes weren't being deceived and then expressed their amazement to me at what just happened.

    It was a pass I learned from seeing my teammate Jake Strong perform it during one of our games when Jake was on my ninth grade Junior Jazz team.

Keep having fun.

That pass occurred in pick-up games at nearby Oak Canyon Junior High School after school because the wood court at Timpanogos High School was under construction for its inaugural year.

A few moments after connecting with my teammate on that pass, one of my knees abruptly locked up to where I couldn't bend it or put weight on it. I had to hop off the court on one foot with my opposite leg and I couldn't play again for the rest of the evening. This is what it was like; one minute or one day being able to play brilliantly and the next minute or day, in a limited capacity or not even at all.

This is the year that I seriously began to lift weights to build up my body. I planned on alternating each day between weightlifting and plyometrics but when leaping, I could not properly lift my legs due to my knees and as hard I worked to complete my plyometric exercises I could not functionally do them. So I made the best out of an extremely frustrating situation and instead, doubled my weightlifting workouts. In the summer of 1997 when we moved to American Fork I was able to gain some improvement in my knees so that I could do the plyometric exercises on the concrete steps outside the house.

The hardest weightlifting exercise for me to perform was the power clean where the weight is on the floor and you squat down to lift the weight up to your chest in one swift and controlled movement. I really struggled to do this exercise correctly. Six years later in

2002, after my knees were repaired from the surgeries, I then could easily perform power cleans.

I didn't make the high school team again for the fifth straight year. I didn't even make the first cuts for the fourth straight year. There were about 50 players who showed up. I had a solid performance during the two days of tryouts in early November but again the coaches barely even paid attention. Frequently they were on the sidelines talking to each other and laughing and joking. They were not taking this as seriously as the players were.

For the season I played church basketball.

1997-1998,
Eighteen years old,
Twelfth grade at American Fork High School,
Six-feet three-inches tall,
Weighing about 175 pounds:

The reason I went to so many schools is because my family had to move frequently. Days after turning twelve years old, we moved from 111 South Eastwood Drive in Orem beside the Westenskows to a house in Provo for eight months, then to a house in another part of Orem for ten months, then to north Orem for four years and then to American Fork.

I finally made the cuts at tryouts for the first time since seventh grade but I didn't make the team for the sixth consecutive year. About 40 players showed up.

The head coach this time did actually watch us

perform and took notes. He paid attention the most since I first tried out back in fifth grade when Steve Downey coached us. I was grateful to finally participate in a tryout where the coach took it seriously.

I played church ball and Junior Jazz until I severely sprained my right ankle in late January 1998.

1998-1999; 2000 to the spring of 2001,
Nineteen to twenty-one years old,
Six-feet four-inches tall,
Weighing about 180 pounds:

I served my two-year mission to Lisbon, Portugal for The Church of Jesus Christ of Latter-Day Saints from January 1999 to January 2001.

I finished growing to reach a height of six feet and four inches.

I worked at Kentucky Fried Chicken before I left and again when I returned.

My knees were surgically repaired in the spring of 2001.

2001-2002,
Twenty-two years old,
Utah Valley State College,
Weighing about 185 pounds:

UVSC held their open walk-on tryouts the first week of April and no one was chosen to make the team from about 70 players who showed up.

2002-2003,
Twenty-three years old,
University of Utah,
Weighing about 190 pounds:
 15 players showed up to the walk-on tryouts in October. I failed to make the team as a player but made the team as one of the equipment managers.

2003-2004,
Twenty-four years old,
University of Utah,
Weighing about 190 pounds:
 11 players showed up in October and I was the "number two man."

2004,
Twenty-five years old,
Last semester at the University of Utah,
Weighing about 190 pounds:

 I'm back again...

 Friday October 22, 2004 at the Huntsman Center. I prayed and asked God to be with me. 11 players showed up including Trevor who has been here with me the previous two years and now he is back again with me for this third straight time at these U of U walk-on tryouts. All 11 players here today in my opinion could play college-level basketball. Everybody was really good. Rick Majerus retired in the spring so we had an entirely new coaching staff this year. And the new coach only wanted to keep one player from the tryouts even though he could keep at least four and maybe five.

We scrimmaged for only about one hour from 7 to 8 in the morning. I was so proud of everyone who showed up and played as hard as they possibly could. It was so much fun playing with so many champions.

I played and guarded all five positions; point guard, shooting guard, forwards and center positions. According to my memory which I wrote down later that day, I made 8 out of 12 shots from the field. Defensively, I held some players that I guarded scoreless including the one they picked to make the team.

In addition to getting low and wide in your defensive stance, if your opponent is a strong outside shooter but a weak driver to the basket, then you get closer to them to take away their space to shoot which forces them to dribble instead.

If your opponent is a weak outside shooter but a strong driver to the basket, then you back slightly away to give them more space to shoot. The increase in space increases the likelihood they will settle for the lower-percentage outside shot instead of dribbling and driving past you because it is more difficult for your opponent to traverse the extra space needed to squeeze past you than it is for you to simply stay in front of your opponent and block their pathway to the basket.

If the right hand of your opponent is their strong hand, then you position your defensive stance at a slant to angle them towards their left so that they must dribble more with their weaker hand, which in this example would be their left hand.

Position yourself to take away the strengths of your opponent and allow them to play into their weaknesses.

We took a break after the first game and the coaches began conversing with one of the players right in front of us. I heard them talking about how this player had a referral, a relative of his, who was a star college basketball player in the early 1990's and who called up the coaching staff to refer this player.

Here we are, only ten minutes into the tryouts and in my opinion the coaches already made their decision of who they were going to choose to make the team.

Minutes later, because I was upset about this development, I unleashed and made an extremely deep three-pointer to make a statement to the coaching staff. I was standing about on the painted Mountain West Conference logo on the left side of the court at about the midway point between the three-point and the half court lines.

It was the most memorable shot of the day.

I heard some gasps of wonder from some coaches when the ball swooshed through the hoop and as I backpedaled back down the court to get ready to play defense.

A member of the coaching staff called me on the phone when I got home later that day. The voice on the other end let me know that I played very well, that he knew I had worked extremely hard, reminded me the head coach only wanted to keep one player and that they decided to go with the player they were talking with after that first game.

    A number of days later I saw Trevor on campus; the same Trevor who also showed up with me to these tryouts three straight years.

    "Trevor!", I called out in excitement.

    "Hi Tim!"

    I was really happy to see Trevor because I wanted him to know how well I thought he played and how great of a thing he has done in coming back every year to make it three straight showings so far. I told him these things and also how great of a person he is for coming back each time. Trevor said the same to me.

    We did it!
    Nothing can stop us!
    No one can stop us!
    Champions!

2005,
Twenty-five years old,
Portugal in the spring,
Weighing about 190 pounds:

    "I don't know what it is about you but you seem to always have that eternal smile," the stewardess said to me on the flight from Salt Lake City to San Francisco. I sincerely thanked her and explained to her that you can't see that quality in someone else if you don't also have it within you.

What she sees is how happy you are when you are going after your dream and you know you cannot be stopped because God is with you as you keep coming back.

I left to return to Portugal on New Year's Eve, flying from Salt Lake City to San Francisco, then straight from there on to Paris, France and then arriving in Lisbon, Portugal on January 1, 2005.

I returned to visit my friends, that we made during my two-year mission four years ago, and to play basketball.

I saved my money in order to carry out this planned comeback of mine. I graduated from the University of Utah in December 2004. I returned to Lisbon. I rented a room that I shared with a roommate from January 1, 2005 until I left on March 31, 2005.

I'm back again.

I tried out with seven semi-pro and professional teams in this order: Algés, Atlético, Estoril, Benfica, Chamusca, Fisica, and Cruz Quebrada. Of these seven, the most professional and most well known is Sport Lisboa Benfica or Benfica for short.

I arrived to Lisbon with a list of teams in the area. I would go straight to the arenas where these teams played, go to the offices, talk to the secretary, get the phone numbers of whatever contacts or coaches I could, try to find a coach to speak to while there, every action I could to try and schedule a tryout. My plan was to hopefully either find a team that needed a player in the middle of the season or sign a contract to play next season.

For example, I went to the arena on January 10 where Benfica plays basketball. I wandered the halls, found someone who worked there, asked them if they knew who the head coach was or when the next practice would be. I got the phone number of the general manager. I called him. I returned to the arena on January 14 to meet the general manager, head coach and an assistant in person. I introduced myself to them in Portuguese and succeeded in scheduling a tryout next week.

On Wednesday January 19 before I left my room, I prayed asking God to help me do my best. At 4 pm I arrived at the arena and warmed up until 5 pm when Coach Alves called the team to gather at midcourt with me included in the team circle to talk about the goals for tonight. I practiced from 5 to 7 pm with Benfica.

We divided into two groups, performed catch and shoot drills. Next we divided into teams of three and repeatedly worked on making five three-pointers in 10 seconds. Bruno and Marc were on my team. We divided into two teams of six and shot free throws. The first team to make 10 free throws wins but every time we missed we had to subtract from our score. I made 4 out of 5 including my last one which was the winning shot, making 10 positives before the other team. Right before I released the ball for that game-winner, one of the players, named Miguel, cheered me saying, "Let's go Timóteo!" (Timothy in Portuguese.) I smiled and hit nothing but net, then I high-fived Miguel and a number of other teammates in celebration of the win.

We got water and then did a number of cut, screen, fade, pick-and-roll, team offensive drills. Next we went three players at a time with one pass, one shot. Then two passes, one penetration, one shot. Then two passes, two penetrations, one shot.

The last 20 minutes of the practice they worked on their plays in preparation for their upcoming game against Queluz. When practice finished we brought the team into a circle for the cheer: "Benfica!"

When I thanked Norberto Alves, the head coach, for the opportunity to train with them, Coach Alves said, "If you want to, you can continue to practice with us."

He said he knew I was looking for a team to sign a contract with and play for and that practicing with Benfica would be good practice for me but it wouldn't necessarily help me find a team.

Benfica has their two foreign players which are two Americans. And in 2005, teams in Portugal could not have more than two foreign players. There were a lot of different rules for regulating the signing of foreign players and this was one of them.

Coach Alves then thought for a second about any teams he might know off the top of his head and told me the assistant coaches would help me. I asked if I could leave my phone number with them and Alves said, "of course."

I left my number with one of the assistants named Nuno. He said a team named Cruz Quebrada might need to sign a new player now so Nuno gave me the name of the head coach there and contact info.

Six of the seven teams I tried out with invited me to keep practicing with them. So I practiced most with the teams that were the best out of those seven such as Benfica and a couple others.

Multiple coaches wanted to sign me to a contract such as André Martins who was the current head coach of Fisica and the prior head coach of Benfica a couple years ago; but since many of these semi-pro teams did not make much money and had complicated rules to signing certain players, it made matters costly for these smaller pro teams to bring on foreign players from outside of Europe.

Benfica though is one of the top basketball teams in Portugal and Europe so the times during these three months that I practiced with them I was playing with some of the most professional basketball players in the world.

It was the greatest feeling for me to hear Coach Alves call my name, "Timót", and I sprint to the spot where he needs me. Nuno, the assistant, throws me a black jersey to put on for the black team and my teammates cheer and support me and each other to each give our maximum effort in winning the scrimmage.

It was the greatest feeling to be part of a real professional team with some of the best players in the world.

The players and coaches of these seven teams treated me with the greatest respect and genuine camaraderie. I really appreciate every player and coach and how much they cared and helped me.

For example, each time I came to practice with Benfica, many of the players would be waving at me as I came walking into the arena with the biggest and most genuine smiles, shaking my hand before and after the practices, and cheering me on during the practices. They were true teammates.

Coach Alves treated me as a true player on Benfica, shaking my hand before each practice and greeting me, "Timót, tàs bom?" ("Tim, are you good?")

I was so happy.

I was there.

My eyes teared up many times with happiness especially when a coach or player would sincerely comment to me on my good play because it felt like God was talking to me through them. I was living my dream during these practices.

We all truly loved basketball and cared about each other. We all knew what basketball is really about.

We all knew what the most difficult and greatest thing you can do in your life is, and who the greatest type of person you can become is.

These players and coaches knew how hard it is for me to be doing what I was doing in trying to sign a contract with a professional team. Many of them have been through the same journey of refusing to quit and to keep going after their dream of playing professional basketball. They knew I was doing the same thing. We all knew what a champion is and what a champion does and this is why we genuinely respected each other so much.

Get back up.

2005,
Twenty-six years old,
Germany in the fall,
Weighing about 190 pounds:

I felt inspired to go to Berlin, Germany to play basketball from September 28 to December 1, 2005 and visit two friends as well.

I went directly to one of the biggest teams in Germany and Europe named ALBA to try and schedule a tryout. The contact in the office gave me the phone number of the public relations manager. I called the p.r. manager and got the cell phone numbers of the head coach of ALBA and Berliner Turnerschaft. I called the head coach of ALBA and left messages but never got a return call. The p.r. manager did tell me that I probably would not get a call back but it was still worth a try.

When I called Frank Müller, the head coach of Berliner Turnerschaft, he invited me to come play in their preseason game tonight.

Frank talked to me before the game and explained he just started this team this year. It's brand new and they have no money. He is coaching and playing for free. It's the first time he's ever done anything for free. He played professionally in the center position for a team in Saint Petersburg, Russia.

Berliner Turnerschaft is a pro team in the lower division in Germany trying to get funding from a couple sponsors to become a team in the higher division which is called Bundesliga and is the same division where ALBA plays.

Frank said he would see what other teams he knows and find out if they need anybody and perhaps I can get a contract with one of them. He said there is more money and teams in West Germany.

We won the game tonight 85-66 against Tus Lichterfelde and I played about 8 minutes.

The next night we had another preseason game that we won by about 5 points. I played the entire second quarter which was 10 minutes and I had some real nice plays on defense and offense again and got some big rebounds.

Afterward Frank came up to me and asked if I was going to be in Berlin for a while? I said, "for at least two months."

He told me the next practice would be Tuesday night and gave me the address.

Practices were so much fun because we were full of professionals who were really serious about winning and helping each other. We usually worked on four different offensive plays called: fier (four), four-corner, horns and head. I practiced with Berliner Turnerschaft until I left Berlin.

I could play in the preseason games but not in the regular season games because I was not under contract. Frank could not sign me to a contract either since the team had no money yet. I would be happy to play for free to get started and then work my way up but the team has to pay other fees and get a work permit when signing a foreign player.

My knees actually started bothering me a lot earlier in the year in Portugal and now in Germany the pain was getting worse. They were frequently swollen. I think the impact on my knees from playing nonstop on a grueling and dynamic schedule and on so many different courts and hard surfaces put a lot of stress on my joints.

I began crying in the subway station after practice one night as I waited alone for the train to arrive because I thought that this might be the end of playing basketball because the pain of my knees was so severe.

When I returned home to Utah I took a break from basketball to rest my knees and prayed that I would be able to come back again.

The fun is in the comeback.

Keep coming back…

CHAPTER 10

GOD IS VICTORY

Our life is about winning the championship.

If God did everything for us and protected us from all pain and suffering and won the championship entirely for us, we would not know what it feels like to win the championship because we did not work for it.

God does not cause any of the pain or suffering, but He does allow it to happen only to a certain degree that we can withstand so that we learn why winning is important and how to win.

You are not alone. God is with you. He is not going to do everything for you but He will help you to guarantee victory if you choose to let Him help you. God is the ultimate teammate.

Do your best and God will do the rest. We have to work for what we want and live by faith in God to guarantee victory.

So when bad things happen and the darkness appears to say, "See, God doesn't care about you. Why didn't God stop this pain and suffering from happening to you?", you know that there is more than meets the mortal eye.

The apostle Paul saw and felt Heaven, where God dwells, as recorded in the Bible in 2 Corinthians, chapter 12, verses 2 through 4. Paul says he was "caught up to the third heaven" in verse 2.

After gaining this celestial perspective Paul then writes an epistle or a letter to the Romans; and in Romans chapter 8, verse 18 we read:

> "For I reckon that the sufferings of this present time are not worthy to be compared with the glory which shall be revealed in us."

Paul is saying that no matter what we go though here during the mortal part of our championship journey or "present time", that no matter how hard or painful; all the suffering we experience will all seem like nothing when compared to what God has prepared and has in store and has waiting for us once we win the championship and triumphantly return home to Heaven.

It is definitely very difficult at the time you are experiencing the pain, sometimes horribly difficult and unfair but when you win the championship and forever triumph it will all be worth it and everything will be made right.

And remember that Jesus Christ, the Son of God, suffered all things. Jesus knows exactly what you have gone through and are going through because Jesus experienced every single pain, every single negative thing that has ever happened to you.

And this is why we cannot win the championship alone on our own and why we need God to help us because God has overcome and triumphed over all things. God is all-powerful.

In the Bible in Matthew chapter 14, verses 22 through 33 we read about when Jesus walks on the water of the sea in the midst of strong winds.

The disciples are out in the middle of the sea being blown by the wind in the opposite direction that they wanted to go. Jesus appears in the middle of the night, emerging from the darkness and walking on the water towards the disciples in the ship. Peter leaves the boat, exercises faith and also walks on the water toward Jesus and when the wind rises Peter becomes afraid and begins sinking. As he begins to sink he calls out to Jesus and immediately Jesus is there stretching out his arm and hand to Peter and pulls Peter back up on top of the water to walk along the side of Jesus and together they return to the ship and the wind ceases.

The water represents the world and all things negative.

Jesus walking on top of the water represents the victory that Jesus has overcome the world. Jesus has overcome all death and all sin, all pain and all suffering, all things negative.

Do your best by exercising faith in God and God will emerge to do the rest that you cannot do yourself, to help you be forever victorious. We exercise faith in God by getting back up, by coming back, by never giving up. Then comes the victory.

God is victory.

The mortal part of our journey when compared to eternity will seem like a blink of an eye. This "present time" is the most important part of all eternity. We are currently in the fourth and final quarter with just minutes remaining in the championship game.

This is the only time we will ever have to experience certain pain and suffering. Not before or after this "present time" do we ever experience the negative things that we do here and then also we will experience turning those negatives into positives, with the help of God. This is our time. This is our time to win the championship.

CHAPTER 11

PETE CUMMINGS: THE GREATEST EVER

Who comes to your mind when you think of the greatest basketball player ever? The best basketball players in the world do play in the NBA, although, the greatest basketball player ever never played in the NBA, or at the college level or on their high school team.

The greatest basketball player ever, Pete Cummings, teaches us three simple and profound truths through his God-given talent of playing basketball.

In the book of John of the New Testament of the Bible in chapter 9, verses 1 through 9, Jesus Christ heals a man who was born blind by restoring his eyesight. The people ask Jesus why this man was born blind and in the third verse Jesus says the man was born blind so, "that the works of God should be made manifest in him." Keep this thought on your mind as we learn Pete's message together.

The second to last time I played basketball with Pete Cummings was on January 21, 2010. On this particular afternoon, Pete was having a hard time making shots from the outside. We played for 90 minutes. And when we play, we play all out hard. Pete must have taken and missed at least a dozen three-point shots.

Although he could not find his rhythm on this day he kept himself prepared without fail for the next good opportunity to shoot. When a good opportunity presented itself to shoot the ball again, Pete was ready and shot without hesitation. Even though he still had not made a three-pointer yet all day, he kept shooting with the same confidence as if he had actually been shooting well all day. He kept playing with the right mindset of teamwork. Pete did not stop.

During the last game when most of the players were pretty tired, Pete shot the ball from the top of the key from well behind the three-point line and made the game-winning shot! It was a big-time play to win a very close and hard fought game.

Even though he had not made a three-pointer all day long he still took that shot with the confidence he was going to make it and win the game for his team.

We said to Pete how awesome it was that the only three-pointer he made all day was the last one he took and also the game-winner!

Truth 1:
Trusting in God, Plus Our Best Effort, Equals Victory!

To make our goals and dreams come true, we need to keep going after them with the same preparation and confidence to make them come true no matter what the circumstances. It does not matter how many times we might have previously failed, just keep shooting with confidence. Heartache or suffering changes in an instant when that game-winning shot is made.

As demonstrated by Pete's actions or exercising of faith, when we trust in God, we receive the power to win. Namely, we receive the power to keep shooting with confidence, to not give up and to get back up when we get knocked down no matter what the odds might seem to be. As long as we do our best by giving our best effort, in God's own way and time, He will help us to hit that game-winning shot!

Truth 2:
Stay On The Winning Team.

Many times in life it can seem to us that God is not really there, that He really is not helping us to win. We keep doing everything we can that is in our control but we keep missing our shots and wonder where God's help is at. Of course we do not want to lose, we want to win. In these discouraging times of doubt we are tempted to change teams because it can seem like we are actually on the losing team.

I was on Pete's team that last game and I was exhausted. Before he took the game-winning shot I positioned myself directly under the basket to get ready for the possible rebound. I remember seeing Pete closely defended as he launched the ball. I could only see a part of his arm as he shot and see the ball as it rose over the defender toward the hoop. It was a very difficult shot. As the ball flew through the air I boxed out the great Dan McMillan for the possible rebound and I remember thinking to myself, "Please go in because I am really tired."

Remember that the game has already been won. Stay on the winning team, even if it may seem like you have no chance to win. When it seems like you are in the fourth and final quarter with very little time left on the clock and the opposing team has a huge lead, stay on the winning team.

God will appear and come out of what seems like nowhere to hit that game-winning shot for you and win the game. Even when you are tired, in basketball and in life, just keep moving forward and God will do the rest in His own way and time.

Truth 3:
God Reveals Himself Through Our Talents.

In playing basketball with Pete, being a direct witness of his talents, and meeting his friends and family, it is so obviously clear that Pete Cummings was born and meant to play basketball.

God has given each one of us divine gifts and talents to fulfill divine purposes. This is as Christ explained so "that the works of God should be made manifest in him," when Christ healed the blind man.

People talk about Michael Jordan as one example of who is the greatest basketball player ever. Jordan used the body God gave him, did his best to cultivate his basketball talents, never gave up and ultimately fulfilled the purposes of the gifts and talents he was given.

Pete Cummings did the same. Cummings used the body God gave him, did his best to cultivate his basketball talents, never gave up and ultimately fulfilled the purposes of the gifts and talents he was given.

Anyone who simply trusts in God by doing their best, does not give up, and stays on the winning team: fulfills their purposes and is the greatest ever.

The account I gave about the second to last time I played basketball with Pete on January 21, 2010 is only one example of how God revealed himself through Pete's basketball talents.

Pete was in great shape. He was usually one of the first guys up the floor on the offensive end and one of the first guys back down the floor on the defensive end.

Pete was such a great passer. I was on the receiving end of many perfect passes from him on fast breaks and pick-and-roll plays. He was a team player from start to finish. He was always trying to cheer his teammates on and look for and acknowledge the positive things each person was doing to help each other win.

There were times when I was also having an off day shooting from the outside and I would hesitate before shooting another three-pointer. However, I would hear Pete's voice cheering me on saying, "yeah, that's your shot Tim," giving me the confidence to shoot again. Then I would knock it down and point back at Pete and thank him for the confidence boost.

Finish the Race Victorious!

One week later on January 28, 2010, Pete Cummings without warning suffered multiple strokes. He miraculously recovered from the strokes just weeks later. As many of his basketball friends and teammates visited him in the hospital we were amazed as we witnessed Pete as a living miracle.

Pete talked about how he soon would be back to play basketball again.

When I met his mother, she said to me that, "Pete never gives up, he never quits."

In the hospital Pete told his family he did not know why these difficult experiences were happening to him but that he was never going to give up.

Pete returned home from the hospital almost fully recovered from the strokes. When he was strong enough, he returned to the hospital once more for his scheduled heart surgery to strengthen one of his heart valves that was weakened when he had the strokes.

During the surgery Pete Cummings suddenly and unexpectedly died at the very young age of thirty-five on April 13, 2010. He is married and has four children.

In this account of Pete's message, I talked about him in the past tense saying he "was" this or he "was" that but there is no "was". Pete finished the race victorious and he "is".

Returning to chapter 9 in the book of John after the blind man is healed, some people did not think the victoriously healed former blind man was the same person. But in verse 9, the victorious man says, "I am he."

CHAPTER 12

MAMA: THE GREATEST EVER

Art is anything that brings us closer to the divine, closer to God. My mother, Kathleen, is the greatest artist ever.

Mama was born to be an artist, among other things she was also meant to do. She painted a huge wooden chest with the McGaffin Five on the chest as bunny rabbits. She painted huge wooden piggy banks and gave each member of our family one. She painted wooden rocking chairs, rocking horses, doll houses, a baby cradle —that Grandpa John McGaffin made and gave to her— and she paints countless wooden lids that fit onto glass storage jars which hold oatmeal, flour, lentils and other food.

Mama hand draws pictures of scenes on birthday cards that tell stories of our family and identifies the individual talents and gifts of each one of us.

Mama writes poems and letters about the greatness of each one of us for our birthday or for Christmas or Easter and Saint Patrick's Day and poems that show and tell us how much she loves each of us and how special each one of us is.

She creates treasure hunts with clues and notes of where to go and look to find gifts and treasures from Heaven.

She makes birthday cakes that are eight layers tall reaching a height of about two feet.

She tape records top secret messages to give us with specific instructions on how to carry out our heavenly missions and fulfill our chosen destiny, goals and dreams.

The greatest divine gift and talent of Mama is her ability and desire to recognize and discern light and truth, follow it, stand up for it, fight for it, and then teach us how to each do the same by recognizing and cultivating that divineness or godliness within ourselves. Or in other words, her greatest talent or power is: to do what is right, to never give up, to be a champion, to follow God, to be a true queen, to be the best mother ever. All different ways to describe the same talent or power.

Victory!

In Mama's own words she describes the victory:

> "When I was nineteen years of age during the summer of 1972 I was seriously ill with hepatitis B. I was very weak and I lapsed in and out of consciousness for days at a time.
>
> I awoke one day and was desperately

trying to sit up in bed. Then, I felt myself leaving my body. I knew I was dying. I pleaded with God to let me live. I prayed to God to let me know what it was He wanted me to do. And I promised Him that I would do it.

Immediately I was healed and I was able to get out of bed.

I hurried downstairs to show my mother that I was healed. She was concerned though because I still looked very sick due to the jaundice of my skin and whites of my eyes where my skin and eyes had a very yellow discoloration.

But I said, 'I feel great!'

I still had the outward appearance that I was sick, but I was not. I was completely healed.

My doctor could not explain my sudden recovery. I did not tell the doctor or anyone about my experience that day in bed.

A number of weeks later I felt a strong prompting to move to Southern California and live with my Uncle Paul. The day I left home in Lancaster, Pennsylvania and said my goodbyes, my mother told me she hoped I would find what I was looking for.

Even my mother knew I was searching for something. My mother and I both cried because we both knew in our hearts that I wouldn't be coming back home again to stay. I left to the West Coast to live with Uncle Paul for a while.

I eventually found a good job in California and needed a place to stay close to my work. As I was searching for a place, Ruby Bodley, a member of the Mormon church, was praying for a tenant to rent out a room. She was praying for someone to introduce to the gospel. She finished her prayer as I drove up to her house in my car.

Ruby became my landlady and I joined The Church of Jesus Christ of Latter-Day Saints. I was baptized on May 1, 1974, the day before my twenty-first birthday. The Lord answered both of our prayers.

In Doctrine and Covenants chapter 112, verse 10 it reads:

> 'Be thou humble; and the Lord thy God shall lead thee by the hand, and give thee answer to thy prayers.'

The Lord has blessed and guided my life wherein the gospel of Jesus Christ has been brought to me. I know I came to the earth at this time so I could accept the gospel. It was not by chance, for it rang true to my ears when I heard it. The Lord blessed me with a testimony.

I met Elder Timothy McGaffin on Monday April 18, 1977 at a sunrise testimony meeting down on the beach. I was serving as a stake missionary for the Torrance North Stake. Elder McGaffin was serving as a full-time Spanish-speaking missionary in Los Angeles, California. We both shared our testimonies on how we know Jesus Christ restored His church in the last days. When Elder McGaffin shared his testimony I knew he was the one to marry and I wondered if he felt the same way!

When we completed our missions, for our first date we saw Star Wars at the Grauman's Chinese Theatre.

We married in the Los Angeles Temple on July 21, 1978.

Throughout my life I've had many spiritual experiences which have strengthened my testimony. The sweetest spiritual experiences I've ever had was when I gave birth to my children.

When my oldest son, Timothy was born on August 23, 1979, I had angels and heavenly beings right by my side who helped me through the childbirth.

When my daughter, Pollyanna was born on August 9, 1981, she was revived and brought back to life by the power of the priesthood.

When my youngest son, Patrick was born on May 31, 1984, the Lord spared my life as I passed through the shadow of death.

My testimony grew and my love for Heavenly Father. I am blessed with children who are the Lord's choice spirits. I am grateful to be a mother, it's what I always wanted since I was a small child."

When I (Timmy) left on my two-year mission to Portugal, Mama wrote down her testimony again of The Book of Mormon and the gospel on a piece of paper to take with me and keep on the inside cover of my scriptures. Here is what she wrote to me in her own words:

> "I have a testimony of The Book of Mormon. When the missionaries taught me the gospel I told them: 'I've been in the wrong church all this time!'
> The Book of Mormon rang true to my ears! I also prayed about it and constantly kept a prayer in my heart for several weeks wanting to know the truth. The Lord answered my prayers that it truly is the word of God. I know that for a fact that I cannot deny.
> His church lives today.
> I say these things in the name of Jesus Christ. Amen."

CHAPTER 13

POPPY: THE GREATEST EVER

I am named after the greatest basketball player ever, my father, Timothy John McGaffin.

Poppy, my dad, played basketball for Bishop Carroll High School in Wichita, Kansas.

In his senior year he guarded the number one scorer in the entire state of Kansas in 1971. Poppy held the highest scorer in the state completely scoreless for the entire game. A feat that could have been seen as impossible but not for my dad who proved once again when you do your best, the impossible is achieved.

The local newspaper in Wichita, called the Beacon, wrote about another game that season in which Bishop Carroll came back from being down 10 points to Mulvane to tie the game and send it into overtime.

The article entitled, "Juicy Conversation Now in Store For Campus Cage Tournament Fans", reported:

"Mulvane had an opportunity to win the game with :06 showing as [Craig] Levering had a one-and-one opportunity. He missed and Carroll's Jim Lewis rebounded, passed to [George] Adams who took a short shot which went astray. McGaffin came up with the rebound and scored to knot it at 52-all."

"McGaffin, a 6-foot guard", the article earlier said describing my dad, sent the game into overtime when he tied the score at 52 when he made a left-handed reverse layup off the glass with his back facing the baseline at the buzzer! The article says on that play with 6 seconds remaining, Adams took a short shot but my dad said the shot was extremely long and my dad saw it was going to fall short so he expertly timed the catch and then the make, at the very last second.

Bishop Carroll ended up losing to Mulvane 56-54 in overtime.

"We didn't lack the effort," said Curtis Hightower, the head coach, when referring to Carroll coming back after being down 10 points.

The next year in 1972, Poppy was now in the United States Army and stationed at Fort Monmouth, New Jersey.

Playing in a pick-up basketball game one Saturday afternoon, my dad brilliantly scored shot after shot after shot as he revealed one of the greatest performances in basketball history. Guys were hanging all over my dad, grabbing and pulling his shirt and shorts and Poppy was still making shots all over the place. Many players who were witnesses this day said it was one of the most explosive and amazing performances they had ever seen.

Towards the end of the game my dad severely injured his right ankle when he sprained, tore ligaments and dislocated it. The injury was so severe that it basically ended the days of my dad playing basketball for years.

Then later when stationed in Okinawa, Japan, doing television equipment repair for the Army, my dad had a friend named John whose wife was pregnant and one night as John was falling asleep he heard a voice say out loud: "Seek ye out the true church."

John turned to his wife and asked her, "Did you say something?"

"No, I didn't say anything," she said. "But I sure heard it."

John decided he was going to ask the first person he saw the next morning what is a good church to go to.

He left his apartment and drove to the television station. He walked into the lobby and there was no one there.

He walked down to the radio side of the station and there was no one there.

He walked into the control room of the television station and there was no one there.

He walked out to where the Okinawans repair television equipment and there sitting alone at the work bench was the sergeant smoking a cigarette and drinking a cup of coffee.

John asked Sergeant Paul if he knew of a good church that he and his wife could go to.

Sergeant Paul currently was not actively attending church and he told John, "Yeah, I know of a good church you can go to." And then told him to go to The Church of Jesus Christ of Latter-Day Saints.

Elder Peterson, who was serving as a "seventy" in the church, which is basically an area missionary, began teaching John the missionary gospel lessons.

John told Poppy what he was learning and my dad liked what John was sharing with him. Elder Peterson then taught my dad the lessons.

John was baptized and then he in turn later baptized Poppy.

Poppy was baptized on March 29, 1975. He was twenty-one years old.

Poppy then chose to serve a two-year Spanish-speaking mission to Los Angeles from June 1976 to July 1978.

He then met Mama on that day on the beach April 18, 1977 for the sunrise testimony meeting.

Poppy arrived to the testimony meeting that morning after Mama and he first noticed her long blonde hair shining and beaming brightly in the sun.

"Where did that missionary come from!", he wondered to himself when he saw Mama.

My dad, when telling me, Polly and Pat about these miracles that happened, teaches us that these things didn't happen by mere chance or coincidence. As Poppy says, these things happened as answers to prayers. Miracles come from God after we do our part and exercise faith (never give up)!

My dad enlisted in the Army because his draft number was three. When you are drafted you have no choice of what you want to do in the Army. But when you enlist you do have a choice. Therefore since his draft number was three, my dad thought the chances were extremely high he was going to get drafted into the Vietnam War and not have a choice so he enlisted instead.

He chose to do television equipment repair and started serving in the Army in May 1972 and next was stationed at Fort Monmouth, New Jersey starting in August 1972.

After about eight months or so passed, the instructors nominated my dad to also become an instructor for television equipment repair at Fort Monmouth. When you are nominated to be an instructor it is basically a 99.9 percent surety that it is going to happen. He was nominated, approved, passed, and signed off on to stay and be an instructor.

The transfer orders came and were read in alphabetical order as my dad listened to where everybody else was going to be transferred to. When the instructor got to John's name, the order was given that John was going to Okinawa, Japan. My dad started laughing since John was his friend and the instructor said, "I don't know what you're laughing about

McGaffin because you're going too!"

Poppy exercised the greatest talent or power there is which is: doing what is right, or recognizing truth and light and then following that truth and light, or exercising faith in God, or never giving up. Four different ways among others to describe the same God-given gift or talent.

Poppy and Mama taught us to always ask questions and never stop praying because God will answer our questions and answer our prayers. God will help us find and understand the light and the truth and give us the power to never give up in following the light and doing what is right.

Poppy is a true king and champion, the greatest father ever!

Victory!

Me and Poppy also both have the same nicknames of "Laffin McGaffin". Some kids were making fun of me at school during recess one day when I was little but no matter what they said or did to me, I kept laughing it off. One of the kids noticed this and yelled out to the others in the group that there was nothing they could do that would bother me because no matter what they said or did to me, —I just kept laughing.

"He's Laffin McGaffin!", the kid proclaimed.

After school I told my dad what happened and my dad said, "that's my name too," and then showed me an old bowling shirt of his with "Laffin McGaffin" embroidered on the back left shoulder.

CHAPTER 14

NEVER NEVER NEVER GIVE UP!

On a weekday morning in November 2009 I had finished reading my scriptures and was thinking to myself about when I prayed when I was little and received the answer to play basketball.

I was thinking about how God promised me He would help me make my dream come true of playing basketball in the NBA and how I still had not made it to the NBA but I still had not given up either. At this moment of thinking these things, Heavenly Father spoke to me in my heart, saying:

"Remember when I answered your prayer, your dream was not to make it to the NBA, your dream was to become the greatest basketball player ever."

I thought in my flawed human understanding that in order for me to become the greatest basketball player ever I would need to play in the NBA. So because of that flawed understanding of mine, I focused on playing in the NBA to make my actual dream of becoming the greatest basketball player ever come true.

Heavenly Father reminded me on this November morning that He had fulfilled His promise to me and that I had already made my dream come true even though I did not make it to the NBA yet.

I am the greatest basketball player of all time.

My prayers were answered!
My dream came true!

Anyone who chooses to do their best and then does their best, wins the championship and becomes the greatest ever! You are a champion.

Never give up or quit on yourself or your dreams because God is with you. Never allow the world to put limitations on you or stop you from going after your dreams.

Never give up and you will always win.

Whenever you are inspired to do something in your life, God has given you a dream to fulfill. God cannot give you a dream without also giving you the power to make that dream come true.

God doesn't inspire you to failure. God inspires you to succeed and win.

The person who can turn any hard or difficult time into something good again and again is a godly quality and this person can never be defeated.

During your journey to make your dreams come

true, you may not always know or understand what the divine purposes of your dreams are that God gave you.

All you have to do is focus on doing your best or in other words, NEVER GIVE UP! NEVER QUIT!

Never give up and you will always be successful. You never lose when you show up and do your best.

Nothing and no one can stop you from doing your best except yourself. You are the only thing or person who can stop you.

The effort is what matters and what God cares about. Perfection is in the effort. Perfection is in doing your best effort.

When you do your best (never give up) you always fulfill the dream God gave you no matter what the world might see or think. It only matters what God sees and thinks of you.

As long as you keep getting back up each time you get knocked down you are fulfilling the divine purposes of your gifts, talents and dreams God gave you to fulfill.

Perseverance, persistence, patience, positivity, proceeding, optimism, endurance, dedication, devotion, determination, diligence, integrity, invincible, moving forward, faith (in God), faithfulness, fidelity, follow through, forgiveness, forever, finish, commitment, consistent, constant, continue, charity, complete, courage, keep, loyalty, love, longsuffering, succeed, steady, steadfastness, staying power, survive, stick-to-it-iveness, relentless, withstand, will (will power), unbeatable, unbreakable, unstoppable!

These are all different words and ways, nouns, verbs, and adjectives among many others, that all describe the exact same power which is the greatest power in the universe: Never Quit!

All of these descriptions when simplified down into their basic elemental characteristics are describing the exact same power in different ways. For example, love is "never quit" too. When you simplify love down into its basic fundamental element it is "never quit".

When I learned through my journey that never quitting is the greatest power, I remember hearing as well that love is the greatest power. I thought to myself that they cannot both be the greatest unless they are both the same power. And when you think about it, they are the same!

One: Faith In God.

You always win when you trust in God and not in your own human understanding. If you rely on yourself alone, you will ultimately fail. If you do your best and trust in God to do the rest, you will always ultimately win.

Two: Get Back Up.

The most difficult and greatest thing you can do in your life is to get back up when you get knocked down.

Essentially, these two main truths I learned along my journey are the same. When we do not give up, we are trusting or exercising faith in God. And when we trust or exercise faith in God, we receive the power to not give up.

You are victorious. You are triumphant. You are a champion.

Champions never quit...

There are so many choice spirits, so many children of God saved to be born at this time on earth. We were saved for this; the final hour of the war that began in Heaven between liberty and slavery, between free agency and tyranny and the final triumph will be for liberty!

    This Is It!

"It does not take a majority to prevail but rather, an irate tireless minority keen on setting brush-fires of freedom in the minds of men."
–Samuel Adams

Spread the message!

About the Author:

Timothy John McGaffin II was born in Provo, Utah on August 23, 1979.

Favorite books or documents include: The Book of Mormon, The Bible, Declaration of Independence, U.S. Constitution, Bill of Rights, any book written by Ron Paul, any book written by Ezra Taft Benson, any book about God, the principles of liberty, or champions.

A Victória É Nossa!

www.ChampionsNeverQuit.com

Timothy McGaffin II (12 years old) and John Stockton, April 17, 1992.

Timothy McGaffin II, October 6, 2005; self portrait taken after playing in second preseason game for Berliner Turnerschaft.

The McGaffin Five from left to right: Patrick (age 1), Poppy (Timothy McGaffin), Timmy (age 6), Pollyanna (age 4), Mama (Kathleen McGaffin). →

Timmy (age 11), Patrick (age 6), Poppy (Tim), Mama (Kathleen), Pollyanna (age 9). →

www.ingramcontent.com/pod-product-compliance
Lightning Source LLC
Chambersburg PA
CBHW061428040426
42450CB00007B/954